About the Author

Hofer was born in the 1950s when Hong Kong was under British colonization. When he was a teenager, his mother took him across thousands of miles to Britain, where he endured a great deal of sufferings. Later, he ventured to Canada for further education. He was pressured to return to Hong Kong due to his critical role as the eldest son and his heavy responsibility to take care of his mother. His mother's stories had continued in Hong Kong, USA and China until she passed away. His life together with his mother was extraordinary and full of adventures.

My Hakka Mother

Hofer Ho

My Hakka Mother

Olympia Publishers
London

www.olympiapublishers.com
OLYMPIA PAPERBACK EDITION

Copyright © Hofer Ho 2023

The right of Hofer Ho to be identified as author of
this work has been asserted in accordance with sections 77 and 78 of
the Copyright, Designs and Patents Act 1988.

All Rights Reserved

No reproduction, copy or transmission of this publication
may be made without written permission.
No paragraph of this publication may be reproduced,
copied or transmitted save with the written permission of the publisher,
or in accordance with the provisions
of the Copyright Act 1956 (as amended).

Any person who commits any unauthorized act in relation to
this publication may be liable to criminal
prosecution and civil claims for damage.

A CIP catalogue record for this title is
available from the British Library.

ISBN: 978-1-80439-306-2

This is a work of fiction.
Names, characters, places and incidents originate from the writer's
imagination. Any resemblance to actual persons, living or dead, is
purely coincidental.

First Published in 2023

Olympia Publishers
Tallis House
2 Tallis Street
London
EC4Y 0AB

Printed in Great Britain

Acknowledgments

Thank you to my family and friends for encouraging and helping me to write this book.

Contents

Preface 11

Cancer 16

Hong Kong 21

Love at First Sight 26

Luk Bo Village 31

Resettlement 36

Little Workshop 44

The Riot 50

Little Uncle 57

Departure 62

Reunion 71

Glasgow 83

Drumchapel 94

Game Over 106

Imprisonment 111

Stanley 116

Land Lady 122

Immigration 125

Chicago	130
Father's Death	133
Retirement	141
Pass Away	145
Postscript	150

Preface

Being an ordinary middle-aged man living in Hong Kong, I've always imagined experiencing life as tasting different flavors in food – sweet, sour, bitter and spicy. Through these experiences, I have learned to be grateful and cherish everyone in my life. I often recall past memories of my late mother at night, her strong and strict words really made us tough and confident to withstand all hardships and challenges.

My mother granted my life and guided me through it. I thank my mother for giving me the chance to experience the sun rises, reoccurring seasons and the different flavors in life. She always taught me to march forward through the darkness without fear and never give up on my dreams.

The memories of her are bestowed in this book. It is full of life surprises and events. Although she passed away almost a decade, my memories of her are still strong and clear. These stories naturally emerge from my memories and with ease I can write them down and share them to the world.

She was born in 1934 and was raised in a New Territories' village in Hong Kong. From my knowledge the people of Hakka originated in remote mountains in Fujian and Guangdong – they mostly immigrated from the North to the Southern parts of China. 'Hakka' in Chinese carries the meaning of 'visitors'. The living backgrounds of Hakka women were always different from other Chinese cultures. Since ancient times, men worked in farms and fields while women stayed home doing housework. It was unquestionable for men to handle heavy labor work while women were responsible for the handy work. In contrast, Hakka women had shouldered up the burdens of both men and women. As well, they had to take on the role of both mother and father. The reason for such a different social norm was because Hakka men focused on education or business. They neither worked in farms nor participated in housework. This had resulted in the shortage of the male laborers. Naturally and gradually, dealing with all affairs in their families including raising their children and taking care of the elderly, these tasks had become major burdens on Hakka women. Under these obligations, Hakka women have been cultivated with many admirable characteristics, such as hard working, tough, brave and capable. Under such a tough and unfair lifestyle, Hakka women gradually became a group of 'strong women'. It was described by an English historian that 'Hakka women are the most beautiful and unique labor-oriented females'. Hakka women had collectively expressed excellent humanities, progressive spirits, everlasting stamina and indomitable behaviors. No doubt about it, my mother was one of them.

My mother could be characterized as the classical model of a Hakka woman, hard-working, capable, confident, strong, adventurous and indomitable. She was definitely a beautiful lady and that why I am handsome too! She discarded the traditional Chinese ideology and broke the restraints of the 'Three obedience and Four Virtues' that defined Chinese female roles. Even well into her middle ages, she still had the courage to travel afar to foreign lands, despite the burden of leaving her family. She was determined to pursue her freedom and dreams regardless of the hardships.

Of course, she strongly believed in traditional Chinese

ideologies. Similar to other traditional Chinese parents, she expected her four children to fully obey filial piety rules at all times, meaning full respect to their parents, elderly and ancestors. Under filial piety, it is frowned upon to disobey or disagree with your parents. Even in adulthood these expectations apply. As her children grew up and formed their own families, she still expected her family to live together under her supervision. However, against her will these expectations did not last as her four children chose different lifestyles.

Ah Ching, the eldest sister was the first one to leave the family. She refused the control and restraints our mother had enforced. She married a Chinese American man and lived in Chicago, USA. She kept in contact with our mother through long distance calls and occasionally came back to Hong Kong for visits while she continued to pursue her own American dream.

Ah Ting, the youngest sister had fully adopted our mother's personality. She was stubborn and persistent to create her own path. She chose the toughest route similar to Romeo and Juliet by running away from her family with her boyfriend at a young age. As a young adult she escaped our mother's restraint and with great difficulty she created a peaceful life of her own.

Ah Mo, the youngest son was dedicated and devoted towards our mother who followed all her requests. He was divorced and has a son. Ah Mo had always felt controlled by our mother and often referred to himself as her servant. Despite being the most obedient child, he was often criticized by her. Even with the constant criticism he stayed by her side, and she often rewarded him with financial supports to keep him close.

Lastly, my Chinese name is Ah Ho, the eldest son, who has to carry the weight and responsibility of taking care of my family as traditional to Hakka beliefs. However, I didn't like to take on this role, she was the boss of our family. I tried to maintain our family's relationships through the arguments and emotional days. However, the outcome wasn't always what I had expected. I really hoped for peace and harmony in the family. I prayed that my mother would adopt the words of God. Even I had dream that she could become a loving mother and gentle wife for my father, but as time passed, I was exhausted from the role to mitigate my family's drama. In the end these were all just my dreams. As the eldest son, I tried everything I could to keep my family together. Nothing else mattered to me more than my family.

My mother had never thought of me as a loyal son. I had often disagreed with her and disapproved of her ways since childhood. Our conversations had never been calm, she would raise her voice as subjects irritate her temper and she would begin to shout to show her dominancy. My mother had never hugged me, no matter how hard I had tried. As a matter of fact, I couldn't recall any warm or harmonious moments with her at all. I've often looked upon the painting by Raphael of Virgin Mary hugging baby Jesus. It has always been my desire to receive warmth and love from my mother; in reality, I have not experienced the love of motherhood.

Mother and Son

While both my parents have passed away, I always cherish

all the wonderful memories I have of them. Eventually, I write this book which objectively described my Mother's legendary and extraordinary life.

Through my perspective writing, I always remember the extraordinary life my Mother had experienced and to express my lingering feelings for her. I do not aim to beautify or exaggerate her stories, as her life had always been flawed and different. Frankly speaking, I wish to capture the real and sincere stories of her life to present to anyone reading my book.

Cancer

In June 2013, stunning news came from Mother: she was diagnosed with terminal lung cancer.

Despite almost being eighty years old at the time, she still spent every day dressing up with colorful clothing and was always high-spirited and energetic. In addition to that, she had had facelift surgery in the United States during her earlier years. No doubt, she misled a lot of outsiders to think that she was only around sixty years old. She was a devoted believer that you have to live an extraordinary and wonderful life. She maintained a very active lifestyle with daily swimming and aerobic exercises and strongly believed she would achieve longevity.

When she returned to Hong Kong from China, I took her through all the medical examinations such as MRI, CT scans and biopsies. We were all emotionally and physically drained and exhausted. As we waited for the results, Mother and my younger brother, Ah Mo, went back to her home in Hong Kong to rest.

Whenever she was at home, she would rest on her couch and watch TV. She would leave it on and allow it to blare in the background and let it play. I believed this was to drown out her loneliness. There was always bickering between Mother and Ah Mo. It often starts with her complaints and one day he decided to record their conversations. This was sent to me:

Mother cried, 'To be truly honest, all of you have never appreciated me!'

Ah Mo replied, 'No way! I have! You've always said this to

us! Mom, you're suffering from depression too.'

'Your father has gone to heaven. He always said I'm an amok! Your eldest brother said I would chop his wife into pieces! You decide which side is right! Is your brother's wife better than me?' she yelled.

'Mom, did you really say that? Why would you compare his wife to you? Will you really pick up a knife to chop people?' he asked.

'Will I? Will I? Maybe one day I will fucking chop you to death!' she continued. 'No wonder your brother said I shouldn't live together with you. Your words are too heartbreaking. The TV dramas always teach us to hold back on our words and be empathetic. What you are saying really stabs deep into my heart, idiot!'

After a fierce quarrel, they calmed down and went on watching TV. She ignored her health condition and picked up a lighter lighting a cigarette. With the cigarette lingering in her mouth, she took a deep breath, relieving her anger and spoke again. 'When I was doing work in take-away shop with your uncle in Glasgow, your stupid brother secretly accused me of stealing. Now I'm asking you, am I the only one that needed and used the money?'

Ah Mo honestly answered, 'Mom, it is wrong to steal. There is no need to steal in secrecy.'

'Don't you fucking understand? I was working more jobs! I've suffered and worked harder than anyone else. What's wrong with taking what I deserve?' she scolded loudly.

'Why didn't you just ask for a pay raise? For them, you're the chef and you deserve more money. You are the boss too!' Ah Mo whispered.

Mother was always sensitive about her reputation and wouldn't admit her mistakes. She said with an exaggerated attitude, 'Am I wrong? Where? All of you keep saying that I was wrong, but I'm the only one knowing I am right. You all are shit. Don't you understand me?' She continued to smoke as she coughed louder and louder.

Stopping for a little while, she took a sip of tea, and then continued the argument to defend her innocence.

She yelled, 'Just get lost! You're not my son but my servant. Piss off! I can pay the taxi driver to take me to the hospital. I know how to go there. Get out! I don't need a stupid servant now!' Even with her cancer she did not lose her confidence and was still arrogant and stubborn.

Ah Mo answered sarcastically, 'Of course. You can make it. You have money, and it's convenient to call a taxi in Hong Kong. It is all up to you.'

Mother proudly replied, 'Yes, even if I go to Taiwan to see a doctor with you, I can speak Mandarin. With money, I fear nothing!'

She kept blaming Ah Mo and said, 'You're my servant, but you're out of your stupid mind! You ignored my demands. I did not want your siblings to know I'm sick. But what do you do? You go and tell your brother, sister and even your younger fucking sister! Why? As my servant, you should be obedient to all my demands! You should've never told them, idiot!'

'Mom, I'm not your servant. I'm just trying to use my own way to deal with this,' he replied softly.

She uttered, 'Don't disturb them. If a servant doesn't listen to his master, it's all wrong! Idiot!'

'If I didn't tell my siblings, sooner or later you would eventually criticize me to Ah Ho. You would tell him that I am not obedient to you, right?' he refuted.

'He is not your brother but your enemy! I will ignore all shit of you!' she yelled.

Ah Mo claimed, 'He is not my enemy, but just like a friend.'

She smoked another cigarette and continued, 'You are such a useless servant. You are so eager to tell everyone so you can get rid of your responsibilities. If I die from this, it's none of your business!'

'I'm not passing the responsibility. That's just what you think,' he replied.

'If I die, don't bury me in an expensive coffin. It's a waste!' she ordered.

'Don't worry, it's a packaged service and many choices,' he whispered.

'Don't bother, I already bought a big and expensive grave in China!' she replied.

'Mom, you're too naive! If elder brother incinerates you, what can you do? You can't do anything after you die. He can do whatever he wants! The dead don't have a say,' he snorted.

She could no longer hold her anger and shouted at him, 'How dare you! All of you are not my children but servants! Monsters! If you dare, just do it! Even in death I would not forgive you! I will curse you... curse you...' she was suddenly lost for words.

'Curse me? Die without a complete corpse?' Ah Mo questioned.

'I will come back to you even in death and haunt your days. Your father was right, before he died, he said he would haunt the rest of my life. This is my karma!' she bellowed.

'I don't believe this shit,' he replied.

'Your brother told me not to speak coarsely in front of his daughters. But why not? It is my right to swear whenever I want!' she changed the topic and said.

'I did not hear that...' he pretended and replied.

The above dialogue was secretly recorded by Ah Mo and was sent to my phone. I did not know the purpose of this recording, but I guess he wanted to show me that even with her sickness she still remains fierce. From these conversations, I noticed that Ah Mo was no longer as obedient as before. However, his lousy and mischievous behaviors remain the same. I've always suspected that after all of our Mother's manipulation, Ah Mo had developed 'Stockholm Syndrome'. Perhaps, he was enjoying being Mother's servant!

Later, my mother ignored my advice staying in Hong Kong for treatment and returned to Zhongshan, China together with my brother. While she looked for traditional Chinese doctors and medicine, she maintained her busy lifestyle with investments in real estate and the stock market.

She was overly confident in herself and her strong healthy body. She believed that once she found a well-known traditional Chinese doctor, she could easily control her lung cancer with Chinese medicine. Never had she thought to settle or rest.

After a long search, she chose to accept treatment at Macau Hospital in the Traditional Chinese Medicine Department. This choice was made due to the convenient traffic between Zhongshan and Macau, China, where Ah Mo also resided.

However, after six months the results proved her wrong; the cancer cells spread to her bones and with regret she eventually returned back to Hong Kong for further treatment.

This was an opportune time for Mother to admit her mistakes, but it unfortunately was too late.

Hong Kong

My mother's maiden family was one of the earlier large Hakka families that moved into New Territories, Hong Kong. They sustained themselves through farming chickens and pigs in Kwai Chung. My grandparents had four sons and two daughters. They lived a simple and self-sustained farmer's life.

Mother was the fifth child, the youngest daughter of the family. She had three elder brothers, one elder sister and one younger brother. Once they had the ability to walk, they were immediately put out to work on the farmlands to feed and maintain the farm.

Grandma, born as a Hakka woman, was the toughest lady of all. She had total authority in the household. There was absolute silence whenever she spoke. She was definitely the heroine of the family, with her thundering voice. I was always impressed by the genetic traits of Hakka women. They are hardworking and are never willing to give up. These traits are deeply inherited by my grandma and passed on to Mother and my aunt. They became the authorities of their individual families after marriage.

Grandma, Mother and my Aunt all worked endlessly for their families, despite having their own accomplishments and journeys, they all shared the same fate of living alone in their old age. Both my grandmother and aunt's husband died early in their lives. Is this a coincidence or some kind of fate that my family is bound to? I've always felt empathetic and saddened by this unfortunate fate.

I did not have the opportunity to meet my Grandpa. Mother

always described Grandpa as the head of the household that loved to enjoy drinks and small talk with his friends about his experiences. He was an excellent sailor and worked for a British and American shipping company for over thirty years. He loved his job very much especially when he raised the anchor and clear blue sea water splashed up in the air. After traveling for over thirty years across indescribable scenery and exotic cultures, his experiences had blessed him with unlimited amounts of knowledge. He returned to Hong Kong for retirement and spent his days enjoying liquor, tobacco and talks with peers, while Grandma and his children maintained the farm.

One day, Grandpa was sick and Grandma fetched him some opium in the hope of easing his pain. It was a mystery as to where she obtained the opium. Unbeknownst to her, opium contained morphine, which could lead to severe damage to the central nervous system in the event of an overdose. This would cause mental issues, respiratory difficulties, or could even be fatal. After taking a few doses, Grandpa's health started to decline rapidly. Knowing nothing about the science of opium, Grandma believed the word of others that claimed opium could heal a variety of diseases, so she just took action without any hesitation. As a result, Grandpa's life was cut short. Perhaps, knowing what she had done, she lived the rest of her life in regret. She continued to live as a widow life for more than twenty years after her husband's unexpected death.

Similar to other families, Grandma suffered through the three years and eight months of the brutal rule by the Japanese imperial army in Hong Kong from 1941-1945. They were dark days for many people during which they witnessed numerous victims of starvation stranded on the streets. She used to tell me stories about cannibalism, rape and killing across Hong Kong in those times.

Grandma's eldest son, my oldest uncle, was a strong and muscular young man. He was always straightforward with undefeated morals and was confident with a strong sense of pride towards his home city. He voluntarily joined the Hong Kong Chinese British Army to fight against the Japanese and protect his homeland. At that time, in fear of the Japanese, Grandma and her young sons were restricted to work solely on the farm. Her daughters, including Mother, were forced to hide at home in fear of the Japanese soldiers. They cut their hair short like boys and deliberately tanned their skins to make themselves less appealing to the soldiers.

During the war period, food shortage became a common fear. With bombs dropped on a daily basis on farmlands and food stores, villagers starved to death in the middle of the wreckage. To defend their limited farmland and resources, our family had to use force to fight off intruders. Grandma had to ensure there was food on the table for her family's survival.

My auntie had married the village chief's son at a very young age. Her quality of life and food were guaranteed by her husband's household. However, this came at a price, as she was married as a concubine. Her husband's first wife resided in China and as a result my auntie traded her comfort of living for loneliness and solitude.

With years of horrific war, peace was finally declared in Hong Kong. Throughout the war, auntie's husband had supplied the Japanese troops with necessities in exchange for Japanese military currency and security. Their lives were worry free and much better than others. However, with the surrender of the Japanese, the dozen bags of Japanese military currency they traded in became useless paper overnight.

As a typical Hakka woman, Grandma was very open-minded and pursued the chances of a better life at all costs. After peace was declared, she immediately sent Mother to high school without any hesitation. This school was taught in both English and Chinese. Mother enjoyed her high school life, which many people did not have the chance to do. Grandma was very proud of her.

The eldest brother was honorably discharged from the Hong Kong Chinese British Army. He then later pursued his job as a senior officer at Hong Kong Customs. With his highly ranked position and decent good looks, he naturally attracted attention from ladies. Very quickly he met the girl of his dreams who grew up in urban Hong Kong. Knowing he fell in love with a nice and beautiful woman, he eventually decided to tie the knot. On the contrary, the different cultures of urban and rural Hong Kong, his wife didn't get along with her mother-in-law. As they could no longer bear to live under the same roof, they searched for another place to live and after the marriage, they scrambled to move out of the big family. Uncle's behavior had severely challenged the authority of Grandma resulting in her feeling disregarded and losing her pride. He was then considered a shame and an enemy of the family and they never contacted each other again. Mother stood proudly by my Grandma's side. She blamed her brother for marrying a siren-like woman, who used her beauty and tricks to manipulate him into leaving the family. No doubt, Uncle and Grandma broke off all ties with each other, even during her last days alive, he was nowhere to be found.

In Mother's teenage years, she had a best classmate called Auntie Fang. They both enjoyed dancing and would secretly dress up for every dance occasion. They reveled in the attention from their surrounding male audiences as their skirts spun with the wind as they danced around the hall. They also loved to take the train to Mong Kok, Kowloon from the New Territories, where they would observe the never-ending hustle of visitors and residents. Sometimes they would enjoy a cheap cold drink like ice lemon tea or Coca Cola in a Hong Kong style café until sunset.

These teenage years were deeply influenced by Western culture and she became more accepting of new experiences and a new lifestyle similar to the stylish young movie star So Lai Chun in the famous Hong Kong film 'Days of Being Wild'.

During the anti-Japanese war, the Hakka people had helped to hide many British soldiers. In return the British Government wanted to pay these Hakka people back by granting them the right to live in the United Kingdom. Therefore, my Grandma's three sons left one by one to seek better opportunities in UK in hopes of achieving more wealth and a better future away from the farmlands.

In Britain, all my uncles worked in restaurants. Occasionally, when they came back to Hong Kong for a visit, they would brag about their success in this foreign land. Mother was always impressed and was tempted to go herself. As a matter of fact, as she got older and realized her opportunities slowly decreasing this temptation grew stronger by the day and she eventually decided to take her sons and younger daughter to the foreign country. Without any preparation she ventured out with her family on a difficult journey. Due to the lack of planning her family suffered through all the stages of immigration without any knowledge and support. For years in Britain, we were lonely and hopeless.

Love at First Sight

After graduating from high school, Mother worked as a doctor's assistant in a clinic located in Kowloon. At that time, she was young, tall, slim and beautiful. She was always well dressed. Her most common outfit was a perfectly tailored traditional Chinese style dress called the 'Cheong-Sam' with a matching handbag. She behaved elegantly just like the Chinese saying, 'When walking by, the fragrance comes with the breeze. When sitting down, the charm is shown up in silence'. While she worked at the clinic, she was often complimented as smart and flexible with good memory and hardworking, definitely a capable assistant. With her good looks and intelligence, she attracted many male admirers. From her past photos, she was undeniably a beauty. If Miss Hong Kong had existed at the time, she might easily have been in the finals or be cast in a movie.

She fully inherited her mother's personality; being stubborn she always spoke her mind, and would point out any flaws in others. She would criticize people relentlessly without considering their feelings. She would always say, 'A person who doesn't accept criticism will never improve, and any sweet words will poison a person!' Often, her strong character made her likely to argue with people whom she did not like. Her pride contributed to her sins as she believed she was the daughter of landlord. She put herself at a higher status and berated everyone. She would favor the ones that offer flattering remarks and obedience compared to those that opposed her. Every now and then, she exposed her enormous ego among her peers and unintentionally provoked troubles. As a result, she fought with others and was once detained at a police station. This was the police station where her life was changed – the place where she found her lover, my father.

My father was a tall and handsome young man, especially when he put on his Royal Hong Kong Police uniform. At that time, he was popular amongst the ladies, but none of them ever got his attention. Once Mother laid eyes on my father, her heart started to beat faster and she was instantly attracted to this man she just met. She thanked the thug she fought with earlier that created the chance for her to meet this man. She had fallen in love at first sight. She spoke softly and gently as they chatted about their stories. When she found out he was also Hakka, she instantly knew she needed to be with him. She began to flirt and in the hopes of attracting this young man. Father, of course, naturally fell for this young beautiful Hakka woman and soon they became lovers.

My Wise and Intelligent Father

Was Mother only in love with him because of his looks? She was so blinded by the idea of her perfect relationship that she neglected to check his relationship status. Little did she know, her lover was already legally married to another woman! Although this woman had left Hong Kong with an English police superintendent to move to America, they were not yet legally divorced. No one knows whether my father and this woman had any children. I've always found it ironic that my father's mother, my grandma was also a concubine, and he was her only son. At that time, nothing could stop them and even with the marriage tied to him, he decided to date this beautiful young woman whom he fell deeply in love with. Why would such a young and beautiful lady, who couldn't bear any grievance willingly be a concubine? As their children, we would never understand their love. Just after several months of dating, they got married illegally. Mother was less than twenty years old at the time and with the marriage being forbidden from the start, there was no ceremony or celebration but only their desire to be together. Without having any ceremony or party, to this day I am still unable to find any photos or proof that their marriage ever existed. They didn't care about any legal documents that would bind my father to her previous wife. There were definitely numerous illegal experiences within Mother's extraordinary life. This might have been caused by her personality or her unwillingness to live simply. She loved to take risks and would ignore the law to achieve her goals. Perhaps, she thought she could live a wonderful life by being free and bold.

In contrast, my Father, a law enforcement officer, would never dare to break the law. He had a strong sense of justice and ethics and could distinguish right from wrong. When he was young, he worked at Taikoo Dockyard as a handyman. The tough and heavy labor work built up his strong and muscular body. One day, he heard about a recruitment notice from the Hong Kong

Royal Police at Main Tram Station in Shau Kei Wan. Ever since childhood, he had dreamt of becoming a policeman and fighting criminals. Fearing that there would be many applicants, he quickly rushed to the tram station early the next morning and excitedly handed in his application. According to my father, there was a British superintendent and a Chinese sergeant at the tram station enlisting young people one at a time. There were physical exams that would assess your height and strength, those who didn't pass this exam would leave disappointed. After all the assessments Father was qualified in all aspects and was recruited by the police force. He then started a new life as a government civil agent.

Shau Kei Wan Main Tram Station

Father was over the moon, having realized his childhood dream – he was a member of the police force! Noticing he needed to work hard for his position, he started to study law, English and

Japanese in the hopes it would benefit his career as a decent policeman. Soon he set a life goal to always work hard, keep being ambitious and to be proud of what he had achieved. There had always been a great contrast in personality between Mother and Father; they seemed to have come from two different worlds. Mother had always been blunt and straightforward. She would judge mainly based on appearances without considering what is beneath. She didn't take marriage seriously and wouldn't think about the meaning it entailed. During their early honeymoon stages, they got along and enjoyed their life together, within the span of several years they gave birth to four children. They were both descendants of the Hakka people and I was the eldest son of this family. As a family of six, two sons and two daughters, most would have thought this family would be happy and blissful. However, misfortune and despair gradually built up as children matured and the society shifted. Without having realized it, life was no longer as it was. Mother's self-centered behaviors and Father's short-tempered personality clashed and intensified the friction between them. In the end, their marriage and family relationship could no longer be repaired.

Luk Bo Village

My grandfather was called Ho Gao. Gao means nine in Chinese. There was never an answer to why his name has the number nine in it. Perhaps he had nine siblings or he was the ninth child. This question may never be answered. Grandfather was the owner of a shipping company in Mui Town, Guangdong province of China, nowadays it is also referred as to logistics. Grandfather had two wives in his lifetime. The first wife gave birth to my father's brother and later abandoned the family. Later, he married his second wife and adopted her daughter. It is unknown whether her daughter is biologically related to him. However, it is undeniably certain that my father is biologically related to him.

Grandfather's shipping company shuttled between his hometown in China and Hong Kong with several Chinese workers and sailing boats. The common dock they used is located in Shau Kei Wan, which was also a common gathering location for many Hakka people. Shau Kei Wan is located at the northeast side of Hong Kong Island. It was originally a bay and due to the land shape being similar to a colander, it was given the name of 'Shau Kei' which means colander in Cantonese and 'Wan' meaning bay. It is also the main tram station to go to Sai Wan and with Kowloon and New Territories located on the opposite side of the harbor, this makes Shau Kei Wan one of the most convenient transport stations in Hong Kong. With the rich sea transport conditions, it was convenient for all sorts of sea transport and trade businesses. The busy bustling British dockyard 'Taikoo' was also built right beside the bay making

Shau Kei Wan more prosperous. Grandfather foresaw the potential of Shau Kei Wan with its convenient and popular location, so he decided to purchase a shop to open his own Hong Kong style cafe. He also bought his ancestral house in 'Luk Bo Village' located at the hill side of Shau Kei Wan. It was not easy for grandfather to have a strong sense of commercial investment knowledge at the time. He could be considered as a successful entrepreneur who built his business from scratch. Sadly, he passed away early without the opportunity to take a photo for himself. The only one photo kept in the house was the traditional family photo of grandma and our family.

I don't know when grandfather moved from Mui Town of Guangdong to Luk Bo Village in Shau Kei Wan. The village had dozens of houses and buildings. The villagers were mainly Hakka people and local fishermen. Grandfather's house had more than ten rooms and gardens at both entrances of the house. My father often spent his leisure time in front of the house underneath the tall trees. You could imagine how carefree and happy they were with their growing business. My Grandma and father lived together in the ancestral house with his elder half-brother and wife – we called them Big Uncle and Big Aunt. It was well known to everyone that Big Uncle had a habit of taking opium, which at the time was a legal hobby for the rich. Big Uncle depended on the rental income of the shop in Shau Kei Wan and his father's shipping business to support his family and to maintain his expensive opium addiction. No one in the family knew where the opium was bought or smuggled from. Later it was learned that Big Uncle had gradually spent all their family's assets.

I was also told that Big Uncle was a martial arts coach, but he didn't teach his family members, so no one knew what he taught. Perhaps, his passion has carried through my genes of loving martial arts, I have practiced different styles of martial arts including Hung Boxing, Judo and Taekwondo. Recently I continued this passion with Wing Chun and picked up my childhood memories. At that time, our older cousin also lived with my father and Grandma. Cousin Shan was the son of my second uncle. Second uncle passed away very early and second aunt-in-law had left the big family and remarried leaving Cousin Shan alone and helpless. Big uncle eventually adopted him and from then on, Cousin Shan lived to serve Big Uncle and Aunt as a servant of the family. Due to being adopted, he had to depend on his uncle for his livelihood and lived his life lonely and miserable.

Under such difficult circumstances, Cousin Shan confronted all his challenges in life bravely. Later, he followed my father and joined the Hong Kong Royal Police. Perhaps it's the same genetics and goals that influenced my Cousin Shan to keep working hard to learn English and law. At last, he became a police sergeant, which was the most honorable achievement of his career. It's a pity that he couldn't share this achievement with his parents as his father passed away early and his mother left him. Although he was highly ranked in his career, Cousin Shan had a very sensitive character flaw. He was impatient and had a fierce temper similar to my father. This could be considered a taboo for both work and life if not in control.

Initially, my father's family lived harmoniously, but the appearance of Mother had changed the dynamic of their relationships. Mother's self-centered, blunt and straightforward personality clashed with Big Uncle and his wife. Their personalities were at different ends of the spectrum and were incompatible, like fire and water.

Life in Luk Bo Village

After Mother moved in, she lived with my father in a small room in the ancestral house, while the bigger rooms were rented for local workers. Big Uncle and his wife were strictly in charge of all the rental income and property management. They took full control of all the financial decisions. Traditionally, the oldest son of the family would act as the father, similarly the oldest uncle was then viewed as the master of the mansion. Mother and Big Aunt would constantly argue over all matters such as cooking, washing, laundry and all sorts of household chores. Mother did not consider any relationship seniority between Big Uncle and father. They would often argue and fight days and nights. On top of that, the strict and fierce attitude of Grandma had turned the relationship between mother-in-law and the daughter-in-law increasingly hostile. Mother's dissatisfaction and hatred slowly piled up and life in the mansion was filled with daily fights and secret back stabbings. I often heard stories about Mother running away from the ancestral house to stay at her childhood home. Her mother was a wealthy landlord and could accommodate her temporary stays. Therefore, Mother would often enjoy her stay at her childhood home before returning to her husband's family. Father loved his mother very much. In order to pay her back the love and care he received from her, he would always be on her side – but this only made the relationship between his wife and his mother even more unbearable. After a few years of this awkward situation, Grandma passed away naturally. I would not know if Mother was happy that her mother-in-law passed away or if she felt any sense of guilt in treating her disrespectfully. Despite the constant arguments in the family, Father and Mother wasted no time and had three babies within three and half years; my elder sister, my younger brother and I. It was not easy to stay in one small room with a family of five as it was always crowded. As time passed, the ancestral house was confiscated by the Hong Kong British Government and in return it was arranged that we would live in a public house in Chai Wan of Hong Kong Island. As a result, our family became part of the lower middle class.

Resettlement

Resettlement Building

In the 1950s, fire disasters occurred frequently in Hong Kong.

These fires were mainly in slum areas with a cluster of wooden buildings. Therefore, Hong Kong British Government had implemented a new policy to build brand new public housing in many districts to resettle the residents. I recall as a child, looking at the first high-rise building we lived in at Chai Wan, north east of Hong Kong Island. It was the resettlement apartment assigned to us after our ancestral house had been confiscated. The building was six floors high and didn't have any elevator. We lived on the top floor and would have to climb up and down the stairs every day. With the daily exercises we ended up eating more and Mother would always have to refill the fridge to feed her hungry little strong dinosaurs.

We lived in the first apartment on the sixth floor, the apartment was about 430 square feet. We were assigned a bigger apartment than others with our own kitchen, but without a washroom. With the inconvenience of not having a washroom, there was a cave in the kitchen floor as a makeshift toilet hooked up to the sewer line. We would have to go to the toilet like cats and dogs.

Rows of small rooms lined the corridors. These houses were so small they seemed to be kennels for dogs. They were roughly 215 square feet per room and with the limited space, residents would cook their meals in the corridors. Each floor had its own communal bathrooms. Every day, you would hear the residents singing and chatting while they showered together. This was a unique moment that you could only witness in Hong Kong's historical public housing.

Kindergarten on the Building's Roof

My elder sister, younger brother and I attended the kindergarten on the roof of the building. At that time, we had no worries at all, all our times were spent playing games after school. What I miss most is playing with marbles and the hop-scotch games. Every morning, we carried our bamboo school bags to attend school and began to learn English, ABCDE, one, two, three, four and five etc.

My Bamboo-made Schoolbag

After we settled down in Chai Wan, my younger sister was born. Several years later, we moved to the Hong Kong Royal Police quarters in North Point. As a western style dormitory, it had the beautiful Victoria Harbor view at the front and the green and flourishing the hills at the back. It created quite an imposing scene, flanked by several other dorms. Protected by a heavy metal gate at the entrance and a guard room beside, the site projected the bureaucratic style of the British Government buildings. We were assigned to live on the tenth floor in one of these buildings. It was our first time to live in a building with elevators. As children, we were all excited and satisfied, even though the elevator only reached the seventh floor and we would have to climb the rest of the way. Our new dorm was much more spacious, roughly 750 square feet, with a front balcony facing the sea. We would see birds flying along the horizon and ships, ferries and junks slowly sailing along the waves. The harbor was lively or peaceful at times, with the beautiful scenery of rocks and mountains as it's indescribable backdrop.

Inside the dorm there was a big living room, two small bedrooms, a kitchen and a bathroom. This bathroom was more civilized than the last and was equipped with a white squatting toilet. The two bedrooms were separated by a wood and glass partition with traditional Chinese floral designs while doorways were covered with cloth curtains. All four kids would sleep on the double-deck iron made bed, with wooden boards acting as mattresses. It was unbearably hard to sleep on. This apartment was our little world where we grew up, slept in, played games and had dreams. Living in this dorm was the closest time we had as siblings. During that time, Hong Kong was just an undeveloped small island, people had been hustling about and many places were under construction and development. Many new immigrants from mainland China sought the opportunity to live in this colony. As we compared ourselves to them, we would feel a strange sense of superiority, as we were children being raised by the Hong Kong British Government and never had to worry about housing, schooling and health care.

Father and Mother were in their prime time and they were filled with energy. Surprisingly, despite their differences in personality, they shared similar parental methods; they would scold and beat indiscriminately! They believed that uncut gems do not sparkle, therefore, we would be treated with violence when we made a mistake. We would be beaten with the handle of a duster made with chicken feathers. This is similar to a duster but also a common disciplinary tool used by Hong Kong parents. Now the feather duster is considered by the Hong Kong Government as an illegal weapon to mistreat children. When we see the feather duster, we automatically feel timid, this is common amongst the young generation of that time. The childhood trauma was forever imprinted in our memories. Besides the feather duster, another punishment was to have us kneel down in front of our ancestor's photos and confess our mistakes. My younger brother and I were the ones who had to do this frequently. Sometimes, when we were kneeling and feeling bored, we would give each other a look and burst into laughter. This often caused a more severe punishment which would be banning us from having meals. Besides the physical punishment, Mother trained our bodies by swimming and learning Kung Fu. I love the famous martial artists including 'Huang Boxing', 'Master Wong Fei Hung' and his wife '13th Auntie'. Then I became a die-hard fan of Bruce Lee, kicking every chance I got and practicing martial arts every day. I dreamed about mastering martial arts and creating my own style of Kung Fu that could defeat all the devils by punching a thousand times within a second. I always wondered why Mother prioritized martial arts over cultural knowledge such as reading, singing or dancing etc.

    Mother had always prioritized earning money and doing house chores. In her spare time, she often argued with my father over any sorts of matter. She was never interested in regular housewife's hobbies like Mahjong. She despised the thought of wasting time playing games and would rather use that time to earn more money. My father was always keen on learning foreign languages, he would listen to audio tapes during his spare time to learn English and Japanese. He also attended language classes on the weekends. Due to his short temper, we were disciplined to be absolutely silent whenever he came home after a night shift so we wouldn't disrupt his sleep. However, boys will be boys and we loved to mess around, so my younger brother and I would always get beaten for disrespecting Father's rules. During our painful beatings, if we whimpered or cried, we would be punished with another round of beating. Our Father's handy tool was his leather belt, it was always convenient and created a deep bruise on our bodies. I always remember the pain caused by that leather belt, especially the permanent small triangle scar left on my left thigh. Besides the physical disciplinary punishments, my parents constantly fought with each other. They would grab whatever was handy to arm themselves in the fight, things like dishes, glasses or bowls were often tossed around in their daily routine. We were too young to consider leaving the scene and would often become unwilling spectators of their vicious arguments. Having to witness their disputes, we would be overwhelmed and hide in the corner. Even with our cries and scared reactions, their arguments never seemed to end. As time went by our emotions were disturbed and weakened.

These fighting scenes happened at least once or twice every month. However, despite their constant fighting they would always make up at night. There would be nights where weird sounds were heard from their bedroom, but these sounds were often covered by their snoring after a short while. They were definitely one energetic and hot-tempered couple. It is undeniable that my parents were hard-working. They were part of an aspiring new generation that was born under the symbolic landmark, Lion Rock of Hong Kong. They were quick in following trends of technology and fashion. Our family had upscale technology such as radios and record players manufactured in England and they enjoyed masterpiece hit songs by artists such as Andy Williams, Tom Jones and The Platters. We would hear the songs so often that the lyrics would come out of our mouths without knowing the meaning of the words. Mother enjoyed dressing herself in the newest fashion trends and traditional Chinese cheongsam. Whenever there was a banquet, she would dress up with heavy make-up to enhance her entrance. To others, Mother was a quiet and modest maiden with a strong and muscular husband. They looked like a perfect couple that people would envy. Who would have ever imagined that they had constant arguments and would throw items at each other every chance they got?

My parents had taught us to maintain a clean and tidy living environment and to always be presentable and dress neatly. My younger brother and I were responsible for cleaning the toilet and polishing all our parent's British made leather shoes. Every time we polished them, we would see cockroaches hiding inside the shoes. As we took the shoe, the cockroaches would jump out and scatter around the floor. Did the cockroaches distinguish that the fine leather shoes were made without hazardous chemicals and were imported? Whenever I cleaned those leather shoes, I would prepare myself mentally by closing my eyes before smacking the shoes. Over time this had become one of my childhood traumas and I could no longer wear leather shoes unless I smacked them prior to wearing them. Perhaps this is a good habit to keep.

Little Workshop

We lived happily in the newly-built North Point police quarter. There were six to seven ten-story high buildings. The quarter was equipped with a football playground in the center and stores within the complex. It was designed to be a small community with all kinds of facilities. At that time, there were new public building sites in North Point. The community was blessed with delicious Guangdong wonton noodles shops. Many new immigrants from Shanghai lived nearby and Shanghai restaurants emerged around the community introducing the famous Shanghai sour and spicy soup, noodles and dumplings to the residents.

Police Quarters in North Point

Ah Ching, Ah Mo and I all studied at the nearby Christian primary school taught in Chinese, while Ah Ting studied at Catholic School taught in English, it is located in the mid-levels of Hongkong Island. Due to her studies in an English school since kindergarten, her English was naturally more fluent than ours. At the same time, my father was promoted to be a sergeant major. There were only a few that could achieve this position at each police station. He felt blessed and believed the birth of Ah Ting brought good fortune to his career. As a result he would constantly show favoritism towards his youngest daughter. Their relationship was the strongest among the family.

Thinking back, I faintly recall my home being a sweater workshop with Mother often bringing back unfinished woven sweaters for final processing. Our jobs were to sew the colorful sequins on to the sweaters and turn them into fashionable sweaters. Mother's best assistant was her elder daughter, Ah Ching. She was responsible for sewing on the sequins while Ah Mo and I were responsible for tearing off the pattern paper from underneath the sweater after completion. We would then pack the sweaters and take them to the deliveryman. Ah Ting was too young to help out therefore her only role was to disturb us as she ran around the living room and watched TV while sipping on milk.

Summer time in Hong Kong is always hot and humid with a daily temperature above 28 degrees. It was like holding a ball of fire whenever we held the sweaters in our hands. Our sweat never stopped falling. Whenever we turned on the fan, tiny fibers from the sweaters would fill up the room causing us to choke. Even with Ah Mo and I being almost totally naked wearing only underwear, the heat would creep up on us and we swept through our underwear. It was definitely our preference to work during the winter than the summer as the sweaters made us hot and itchy.

Several years later, Mother and Ah Ching had turned into masters at sewing sequins and stringing beads, while Ah Mo and I had become experienced workers in removing the pattern paper underneath the sweater. With this little workshop, our monthly income increased and slowly our lifestyle reflected this pleasant change. We started to see new electric appliances around the house and had a telephone installed. Mother bought an electric cooker while Father bought audio equipment including a hi-fi and radio. Eventually an air conditioner was also installed in his bedroom without us even noticing when the installation had begun. My father indulged himself in British and American pop music. He had always been fond of British and American products over locally made products. He believed that western goods surpassed in quality. The very first black-and-white German made television installed in our home was put in the living room. Every night we would sit together in the living room to watch television. The well-known Hong Kong TV program called 'Enjoy Yourself Tonight' was our must watch show, it was broadcasted at half past nine every evening. Watching 'fatty' Lydia Sum singing and dancing along with many beautiful superstars would be our favorite entertainment. We would often fall asleep on the couch as the program played in the background. Television was the only free and interesting entertainment we had available to us at night. During that time, Japanese TV series were also gaining popularity, such as 'Volleyball Young Ladies' and 'The Judo Fighters'. 'Volleyball Young Ladies' was one of the classic sports dramas aired, it was launched on Hong Kong TVB in the late 1970s and gained mass popularity among audiences. Many people began to learn to play volleyball in an attempt to imitate the famous actresses' moves.

    The Japanese pop star Su Youmei's beautiful features had captivated me fully. She was truly stunning with her big eyes and high nose, she became my dream girl. I even cut out her movie posters from magazines and stuck them to the wall. I also admired the master in 'The Judo Fighter' and he influenced me to join our judo class in my high school. It had become my teenage life goal to pursue my dream girl and become a judo master.

My father purchased a new red Volkswagen beetle with his accumulated wealth. This tiny car was only equipped with two front doors and the four of us would have to squeeze into the back seat just like tiny beetles. This car brought our family closer together.

My Father's Beetle

Our father enjoyed bringing us on family drives. On holidays we would drive from North Point to Shek O Beach in the south of Hong Kong Island. This was the best family entertainment on weekends. The drive was about half an hour from home, we would admire the scenery along the drive with hills and the ocean speeding past us. We would sit in the back seat enjoying the cool and refreshing wind blowing against our hair and faces. Shortly after, Father began to teach his wife how to drive. Whenever Mother drove, Father would criticize and scold her every move during the whole ride. Nevertheless, as a famous Chinese idiom states 'a strict teacher fosters outstanding students'. These weekly arguments continued from our home to our destination and we once again became unwilling audiences as we watched their constant disputes.

No matter how many quarrels they had, every weekend we would still go to our favorite Hakka restaurant as a whole family. We would enjoy Hakka dishes, such as salt baked chicken, steamed pork belly with preserved greens and fresh bone marrows with seafood etc. After a satisfying dinner, we would go home fulfilled and have a good night's sleep. After a while, Mother surprisingly bought a second-hand British made wagon. Bearing an especially long body, the car could hold up to eight or ten kids. She claimed that the purpose of this vehicle was to chauffeur children to primary school. The production of the sweater workshop began to decline, so Mother had assigned Ah Mo and I some new tasks. Besides the leather shoes polishing and toilet cleaning, we also had to be responsible for cleaning those two vehicles. We had become the servants of our household. From then on, I learned the exact procedure of how to clean a car. We would wipe away the dust, clean out the garbage, wash the body and finish with waxing. After cleaning, our parents happily drove through the streets with a clean and shiny car. Unfortunately, Mother was in a terrible accident. Luckily, she was unhurt. Perhaps, this was because Mother's driving skills were not as good as father's. The damage cost was hefty for the family. Due to this accident, Mother had to stay home. While she was home bound, she began to brainstorm new ways to earn more money!

The Riot

In 1967, Ah Ching studied at a famous middle school in Shau Kei Wan, while I was in fifth grade. I remember a classmate offered me a gift which was a small badge with a middle-age uncle's portrait on it. I pinned it onto my shirt and headed home. I showed it to Mother and she was shocked at the sight of the badge. The next thing I remember was getting beaten and punished to genuflect for hours. Later on, Father returned home and saw the same badge, once again I received another beating by his leather belt. My father shouted a series of unknown words to my face and knowing nothing about the man on the badge. I had no idea the reason for these beatings. This incident was carved deeply into my memory, as I didn't know why I was punished or the meaning behind the badge. I was heartbroken and to this day I can still remember that incident clearly in my mind. In that same year, a gentle and beautiful English teacher came to our class. At the first sight, I was entirely enamored by her. One day, she asked two classmates and I to stand up, I was happy to be called upon. She pointed at the first classmate and said, 'Dirty' while the other one 'Dirtier'. Lastly, she laughed at me and said, 'the Dirtiest!' I smiled and asked her, 'What is the dirtiest?' and from then on, every time when I came across this teacher, I would be reminded of her smirk and how she laughed at me.

One day, our father suddenly disappeared and we lost contact with him. Mother cried all day long and she couldn't keep her temper under control. We did not know that there was a serious riot until we watched the television and heard the news from the radio. Due to the riot, school hours were shortened.

Every time we returned home there would be guards at the metal gate. They were armed with two machine guns pointed towards the entrance of the gate. We were required to declare our residency and our father's identity in order to enter the premises. Apart from attending school, we could only play and buy supplies within the scope of the police quarter. The police increased the amount of police trucks and patrol cars within the area. Most of the goods and supplies were transported directly to the store and distributed to the police families. Some days later, Mother finally caved and told us, 'Your father has become the Captain for the anti-riot police. He won't be coming back anytime soon. There are lots of bombs outside and it is extremely dangerous! You must all come home immediately after school and you can't play outside!' Hearing that, we nodded our heads. There were constant broadcasts about the riots everywhere. In the midst of fear, a lot of rich residents of Hong Kong decided to leave.

Eventually, father returned home. We were all relieved to see him, however despite not seeing us for days, he didn't seem to care. Mother started to persuade him to resign from the police force as she feared it was too dangerous and tough. She tried her best to convince him to move to England, where her brothers were living. Father kept silent, listening and eating at the same time. After he finished the meal, he headed out again. He would only show up at home during daytime, mainly to freshen up. The depressing situation lasted for almost half a year. The riot was initially a labor campaign, however as tension built up and it evolved politically into bomb attacks against the Hong Kong British Colonial Government. During this riot, the entire Hong Kong police force had to cancel any unnecessary leave, to be put on standby as they were assigned to disperse and arrest protestors in more serious situations. At last, eight hundred people were seriously injured and over fifty deaths, including at least five policemen. This riot is a historic turning point in Hong Kong's development. As a result, the Hong Kong British Colonial Government changed their policies in hopes to improve the administration and Hong Kong's welfare system.

The riot gradually quieted down and we were relieved to see our father come back home without any injuries. Due to his excellent performance during this incident, father was assigned to be an instructor at the police academy in Aberdeen. With the rich experience he collected during his anti-riot duties, he got a promotion and received numerous awards. That same year father was promoted to instructor, I too was accepted into a famous English taught Catholic School located in mid-level Hong Kong. During my entrance exam, I saw a girl who resembled superstar Li Sze Kei. She was crowned Miss Hong Kong in 1968. She instantly motivated me to do my best in the exam. I was really determined to get accepted into this school. Unfortunately, this school divided its classes by gender and I never got the chance to see her again.

The Riot in 1967

After father experienced the violence of the riot, his personality had changed slightly. He started to restrain his hot-tempered behaviors and as days went by, he stopped using his discipline tool on us. Although he would still get furious and yell at us, he no longer brought his belt into the fight.

At the Catholic High School, there was a discipline teacher called Mr. Lam. He was short and squat, we often joked and called him 'Fat Lam'. He resembled my father's previous violent behaviors and would imitate western cowboys and swing the thread with a metal whistle. Every time he disciplined the students, he would swing his whistle and the student would endure unbearable pain, the pain was similar to the beatings I had received from my father. All the students were scared of his footsteps. He was the worst teacher I've encountered in my lifetime. He was really an asshole and violent teacher! From the movies I've discovered that Bruce Lee was one of the strongest Kung Fu masters. At a young age, he achieved great power and skills in martial arts from his master, Ip Man in Hong Kong. I strongly remember his theory 'Be Water' where his Kung Fu was so fast and smooth making it one of a kind. I made up my mind to learn martial arts well, in the hopes of going against Fat Lam.

I began to practice 'Hung Boxing' every day and finally one day my chance to go against Fat Lam emerged. I came across Fat Lam in the playground while he was swinging his whistle at my classmate. I caught his whistle with my bare hands. Bingo! I thought. He was so shocked he asked me to stand still. He took a good look at me and said, 'Feeble boy! How dare you!' With all the anger built up, I questioned the eligibility of my school. Why would a famous Catholic school allow a teacher to abuse his students violently? What are they doing in the name of God? Without my noticing he swung his whistle and it hit on my butt.

The pain was so arching that I still recall it whenever I think of the high school!

My middle school years were not a smooth experience. I was assigned to a stubborn and traditional Chinese teacher, who demanded his students memorize every single Chinese character without understanding the meaning behind the text. I started to despise learning Chinese and hated reading textbooks. As a result, I failed all my Chinese subjects including literature and history. My grades were below average and I was eventually forced to repeat that year. Deep inside, I knew I hated this school. I didn't experience any satisfaction or achievement when I studied there. Despite being a Catholic school, I never experienced the benevolent beauty of the kind-hearted Virgin Mary nor the blessing of the Almighty God. I couldn't stop myself from feeling hatred and fear towards this school. Eventually, my father noticed my worrisome expressions and decided to transfer me to another Christian middle school in Stanley. The famous Wing Chun master, 'Ip Man' also attended this school before. Knowing this, I was honored to have the opportunity to study at the same school and strive hard to improve my education.

Not long after that, my father purchased his first home in Stanley. Our family moved into the new home and it became much more convenient for me to walk to school. Stanley was located in the south of Hong Kong Island just by the ocean. Ah Mo and I would often go for a swim after school. There were times where we would swim from the beach near our home to the other side. Stanley is totally different from Hong Kong's urban lifestyle. The life there was simple and peaceful, without the noise of trams and vehicles driving endlessly around the city. We wouldn't hear the sound of residents playing Mahjong or the sounds of busy city night life. The residents of Stanley live a simple and peaceful life and similarly we began to adapt to their lifestyles. However, when weekends come around, urban citizens would flock to Stanley to get away from their city life. They would storm into the tourist areas with beautiful ocean scenery and local restaurants. Stanley eventually developed an area for tourists to visit during the weekends.

Our Home in Stanley

A lot of happy memories were created in Stanley. We could fully enjoy the sunshine, beaches, waves and natural environment it offers. I loved swimming, hiking and overlooking the endless Pacific Ocean. Standing by the sea and staring at the distance, I would watch the large cargo ships sailing forward slowly until they disappeared into the coastline. A group of young children would play along the seabed freely and carelessly. With the sea wind blowing against me, I immersed myself in the peace and beautiful environment.

Little Uncle

We have three uncles on Mother's side. The youngest one, Uncle Hon, followed his brothers, Uncle Hing and Shing to the United Kingdom at a young age. During Japanese army occupied Hong Kong in World War II, many Hakka villagers secretly hid British soldiers in their homes. As gratification, the British Government granted the right of abode to the Hakka people, meaning that an individual was entitled to live and work in the United Kingdom without any restrictions or conditions of stay. Many young Hakka villagers took this opportunity and immigrated to the United Kingdom. As a matter of fact, it is well known that Hakka people aided in rescuing British soldiers, although I do not have proof of Mother's village participating in such a rescue. Perhaps, they were lucky enough with such an opportunity to live in Britain. Undeniably a golden opportunity, my uncles without a doubt, abandoned their farmland and lived in England. Immediate after, they all became British citizens with very little knowledge of the language. Without the linguistic abilities, they were limited to kitchen work, away from the need for any communication with customers. After a few years, to everybody's surprise, Uncle Hon came back to Hong Kong for a visit with his newly wedded Caucasian wife. Uncle Hon was taller than most of us with a sharp defined nose. Most would consider him to be handsome and inspiring. Some even claimed he shared similar facial features with the famous Hong Kong actor Andy Lau. Perhaps, the change in the living environment in England had caused his skin to become much fairer and paler than before. As for his wife, she was Caucasian, born with fair blonde hair and bright blue eyes. Similar to Uncle Hon, she had a slim and slender figure. She was our very first foreign relative. Later on, our Cousin Wai who studied in England also married a Scottish lady. From then on, Mother's family had strong ties with the United Kingdom.

Mother could only speak simple phrases in English such as 'hello', 'how much' and 'bye-bye'. She lacked the ability to communicate with her sister-in-law. Thus, the only thing she could do was smile. Mother would chat with Uncle Hon in the Hakka dialect, and their subjects always revolved around his life in England. Uncle Hon encouraged Mother to go to England, claiming that it is more financially beneficial to earn pounds rather than Hong Kong dollars. He was very pleased with the quality of life that England offered. Mother took Uncle Hon and his wife to all the scenic hot spots, such as the Peak and the Repulse Bay. I accompanied them just like a puppy following its owner. Before they left Hong Kong, Mother even organized a farewell banquet and invited all her family members. My grandma was still alive and in good shape at that time. All of our cousins would greet her one by one as they showed up. It was a pleasant and heartwarming family gathering. During the banquet, Uncle Hon kept repeating how happy he was in England and that all of us should have the desire to go, especially Mother. His wife on the other hand, didn't understand a single word in Hakka. She would watch her husband brag to his relatives not knowing what he was saying. She had devoted her whole evening to enjoying the Cantonese cuisine to its fullest as she was unable to join in the conversations.

Our Cousin Ming's father, also known as Uncle Shing had also followed Uncle Hing and Uncle Hon on a ship to England.

During the banquet, Uncle Hon mentioned that the cheapest fare to England was the lowest-level cabin, which originally was to store cargo or diesel. After a cheap renovation, it became a deck for passengers. Without any windows, you could not see the outside at all. Crowds of people would gather there with nothing to do but sleep or eat. The air was always stale with very little ventilation. When winds and waves were violent, the passengers would get dizzy and it often caused nausea or vomit. It was a harsh journey that took more than one month before reaching the English shores. Their adventures always inspired us and they were our heroes indeed! Cousin Ming was working as an automobile salesman in Hong Kong. Similar to Uncle Hon, he was tall and slim, with a gentle and mellow personality. He never strongly voiced his opinions to others and would prefer to follow the crowd. He was single at that time and lived with his younger brother, two younger sisters and his mother in Hong Kong. His two sisters were called Six Mei and the younger one called Little Mei. Little did I know at the time, that they would eventually betray our family in Scotland. During our family gathering, both Cousin Ming and Mother were particularly excited to learn about earning money in England. They were drowning in information offered by Uncle Hon, that kept them awake the following night. They fantasized the moon being rounder and bigger in the United Kingdom and dreamt about earning quick and easy money. Ever since Uncle Hon left Hong Kong, a common topic was often brought up at the dinner table – how would Mother immigrate to the United Kingdom?

Because of this constant desire to go to the United Kingdom, our parents would argue day and night, most times resulting in bigger fights. Eldest sister would join in the debates, yearning for the chance to study abroad in Canada. With the wife so desperate to go to England and the daughter dreaming about studying overseas, my father, even as a royal police major sergeant could not handle the constant nagging and whining. It was a big pain in the neck! He had no clue how to handle these difficult demands from his two overpowering Hakka women. After several months of continuously battling, my father surrendered. Mother began to gather money for her trip to the United Kingdom. My sister, joining in the party, also achieved father's consent to study abroad in Canada. By making use of the police authority, Father borrowed money from his rich friends for my sister's first year tuition and deposited it into her bank. He said to his eldest daughter, 'Ah Ching, my abilities are very limited, this is the most I can offer you. When you arrive in Canada, you must support yourself, earn money and keep up with your studies!'. She nodded her agreement. Being a part of Hakka people and bearing their strong, independent women genetics, she finally left Hong Kong with nothing to fear. She was the first member to leave our family. I didn't feel any sorrow for her leaving, but I felt the impact it had in our home. It was much quieter after her departure. Mother eventually saved up enough money to be able to afford the expenses of starting her new life in the United Kingdom. With her personal savings she figured it would last her quite a while in the UK. On top of that, she had the help of her brothers. With the safety net in place, she left Hong Kong without any worry in her mind. During the time she prepared to leave, she also persuaded Cousin Ming to leave with her. Cousin Ming did not have a lot to lose in Hong Kong, he was single and didn't have many worries in life. With both Mother and Uncle Hon's repeated persuasion, Cousin Ming eventually caved in and agreed to travel with Mother. They both have one goal in mind- to make a fortune.

  With Mother gone, Father didn't have a choice but to stay home and take care of his two sons and his youngest daughter.

Ironically, I felt that my father might have felt happier without the constant nagging from his wife. Several months before going abroad, Mother said to Father, 'You must submit for an official divorce with your ex-wife. I want an official marriage certificate! I must be your legal wife! Without a legal marriage certificate, our children will never be able to apply for overseas education funding from the Hong Kong police welfare. As children of an illegal marriage, they have to work twice as hard to be able to study abroad!' Father never gave any response. It's possible that Mother knew deep in her heart that father was a dissolute man. She was so brave to venture out on her own, but I always wondered if it ever occurred to her that her husband might meet another woman during her absence? After many years of nagging, Father finally applied for the marriage certificate. However, life played a game on them and they also applied for divorce in their later age where they continued on their wonderful and happy life on their own. I am curious whether the freedom in thought and lifestyle from the British influenced our whole family. Perhaps, freedom always carries a price and for us, it is the members of our family being separated and scattered around the world.

Departure

Mother left Hong Kong with Cousin Ming hoping to pursue her dream in the United Kingdom. During the same year, my elder sister was taking preparatory courses in Windsor, Canada. She was preparing for her university entrance exams while the rest of my family stayed in Hong Kong. Mother spoke to me right before her departure, 'My son, you're the oldest one now. Behave yourself and study hard! Don't chase girls, okay!' I didn't know how to respond to her and I simply muttered one sound, 'Or' that means I got it. I promptly thought who will cook for us!

After Mother left Hong Kong at Kai Tak Airport, it was strange that I didn't miss her, but instead enjoyed the peace at home. I felt free and calm. In my spare time, I went shopping and played with my classmates. I didn't need to go back home on time or have the orders to finish any household chores. Sometimes, I would cook when I wanted or I would order take out. I got to make the decisions where I felt free and happy! Soon I had adapted to a wonderful independent life and it was probably God's plan to prepare me to stay independently oversea in the future.

Hong Kong Kai Tak Airport

At the beginning, Mother wrote letters back home quite often. Father briefly told us her situation in UK. After they had arrived in England, the Immigration Office gave them a tourist visa for six months. Without any hesitation, both Mother and Cousin Ming disregarded the immigration laws and started to work hardcore at a restaurant illegally. They wanted to start earning Pounds immediately.

Taking a train to travel from London to Glasgow, Scotland, they went to visit Mother's younger brother, Uncle Hon, in hopes of depending on him on their tough journey. At that time, Uncle Hon had just divorced his Caucasian wife who had accompanied him on his visit to Hong Kong. He remarried a traditional Hakka woman from the new territories of Hong Kong. The new auntie spoke like a machine gun and she would never stop talking. Her nickname was 'Cannon Sister' because of her forceful and aggressive character. No doubt, it was easy to foresee that Mother and this Cannon Sister didn't have any possibility of getting along well with each other. As a result, Auntie introduced Mother and Cousin Ming to work in another small town called Motherwell. They lived close to the Chinese restaurant they worked for.

As a man of striking appearance, Cousin Ming, communicated with the local Scotts in English with a Cantonese accent, chose to work as a waiter in the restaurant. Mother on the other hand, had to wash bowls and dishes in the kitchen for eight to ten hours a day. This hard-working daughter of the Hakka village chief, endured loneliness in a foreign land and overcame the physical tiredness to show her extreme potential. According to Mother's character, she would definitely not be willing to suppress her talents in the repetitive day to day dishwashing jobs. It was boring, labor intensive and she earned less money. She made up her mind and had strong ambitions to become a restaurant owner. Not long after, she began to learn cooking techniques from the chef. She cooked with the heavy cast iron wok that weighs almost four to five pounds daily and she would also stay busy in the smoky kitchen day and night practicing her arm strength and cooking skills.

Mother in the Kitchen

In fact, the so-called Chinese Cuisine in UK was altered to fit the taste buds of the British people. They often prefer strong flavors and aroma. The real Chinese cuisines had obviously changed in UK, such as Chicken Chop Suey, Shrimp Fried Rice, Sweet and Sour Pork and Curry Chicken etc. All of them were local cuisines modified from Hong Kong Hakka people. Every dish, as long as it's added with MSG and salt, would taste flavorful and delicious for those local people. It's really such a strong taste! Not only that, they would also enjoy their so-called Chinese cuisines with soft drinks or beer and eat their favorite meal with a fork! Three to four months later, Mother had learned the basic cooking technique and was promoted to a deputy chef, responsible for frying and cooking. They usually called the deputy chef, 'Wok Master'. Being responsible for two stoves at the same time, she demonstrated her flexible and quick hand in which she could finish a dish within a minute. The boss of the restaurant admired her very much. As a hard-working lady, she soon became a wonderful chef who earned more money. Every week when she received her salary in cash, she would be filled with joy. Gently touching her wallet full of pounds would make her smile, while she planned in her head on how to fulfill her dream in starting her own restaurant. After being a waiter for months, Cousin Ming learned how to hold three or four dishes with the right hand and two or three bowls of rice with the left hand, just like a circuit player serving his customers. Many female customers dining in the restaurant were attracted to him. Occasionally, the drunken women took advantage of him and touched his butt! By the way, we also learned that one of his colleagues at the restaurant was also indulged with him. This colleague was a Hakka young lady also from Hong Kong, who had gone to UK much earlier. Although both her figure and personality were excellent, Cousin Ming did not fall in love with her. Mother always urged Cousin Ming not to be so stupid since she could be his ticket to becoming a legal immigrant. Then, he would easily start his family right here.

  Mother and Cousin Ming had almost forgotten that they were illegally working in the restaurant. In fact, they did not care much. When their tourist visas were near their expiration dates, they had even been overtaken by the mood to travel to France for a week. They roamed in Paris, went to visit Eiffel Tower, Avenue des Champs Elysees and the Arc de Triomphe and enjoyed coffee in the streets. They even sent their colorful photos back to Hong Kong. When Father showed us those pictures, we couldn't help being amazed by the enviable scenery. We also noticed that both of them had gained weight.

Eiffel Tower

After a week, they returned to UK. To everyone's surprise, the immigration officer gave them another tourist visa for six months. It's a mystery to me how Mother had her visa extended, she might have used her charms and persuaded the officer. Either way Mother had made a breakthrough luckily and succeeded. They started working in Glasgow again. With the ease of extending her visa, Mother thought even the Immigration Office could not do anything to her, she became more arrogant and was obsessed with money. Totally abandoning the thought of working illegally, she decided to stay in UK for good. Out of the blue, she thought of a despicable idea-requesting my younger sister and I to go to Scotland to help her. Obedient children were probably cheaper or even free laborers for her. Mother didn't care whether my younger sister and I were happily going to secondary school in Hong Kong. She called and said in a gentle and unfamiliar tone, 'Come on! Your mother is waiting for you, good boy and girl!'

In Hong Kong, as I entered my teenage years, I started to make a lot of good classmates at my new school, including the attractive girl, the prefect and other nice classmate girls. Most of them treated me well and in return I pretended to be cool and funny to keep them assumed. Every day, I went to school happily, making jokes and babbling to my peers. I enjoyed my rising popularity amongst the girls and was truly happy with where I was in life. English, math and chemistry were my strongest subjects. I would often help tutor my fellow female classmates on the homework in these topics. In my spare time, I had joined the American Air Cadet Association. I constantly dreamt about flying in the air while I wore my air force uniform. Looking in the mirror I could almost see a resemblance to Tom Cruise or Bruce Lee! I was super proud of who I am becoming! The Air Cadets gathered every Saturday, it was my most anticipated day of the week. As I learned about flying techniques and various pilot knowledge, I would always daydream about soaring in the blue sky with my wings spread wide open just like a bird rising past the white clouds. I also had the chance to learn group marching and attended several challenging physical activities. I managed to achieve excellent scores and was invited to visit the giant U.S. aircraft carrier. These experiences were so special and unique to me, I could recall every single one with great familiarity.

American Air Cadet

Of course, good times didn't last in my family, this happy moment soon came to an end. Mother's recent call to my younger sister and me was not a joke, we were going to Scotland. She didn't give any thought into what we were abandoning and pressured us to leave immediately. It was so weird to us that my Mother only requested my younger sister and I to join her. She disregarded my younger brother. I will probably never know her reasoning behind this. During that time, my younger sister was studying in a famous Catholic middle school. Evidently, she was fluent in English and received high marks from her teachers. My younger brother on the other hand would always hover around the minimal passing marks. Like my Mother, he spoke before thinking and was fond of criticizing his peers. Despite his low marks, he always thought he was the best. Compared to me, he cared a lot more about his fashion and his looks. Sometimes, I would think my younger brother was not masculine like traditional men. He didn't enjoy Kung Fu or sports, instead he spoke like an old lady selling vegetables in the market, gossiping and bickering at others. Perhaps, it was because of this, Mother didn't ask him to come with us. I don't remember the day when he finally joined us in Scotland, but I barely remember him being the last one to leave Hong Kong.

Reunion

Under Mother's authoritarian-like pressure, Father caved in again. Despite the protests from my younger sister and I, he agreed to fly us to UK, removing us from our perfect teenage life in Hong Kong. Several weeks before leaving, I could feel Father's love and care. He took me to the famous local watch shop and introduced me to his good friend who was its owner.

With Father's deep voice he told his good friend, 'My eldest son is going to study in UK, I want to buy him a new watch before he leaves.'

Almost immediately, the owner brought over a luxury Swiss watch. Father quickly rejected it and said, 'Not the Crown brand! It's too old-fashioned!' He nudged me and said, 'Son, choose yourself.'

Since I loved swimming at the time, I decided on the Omega diving watch. The sports style matched my character and I secretly fantasized myself as James Bond. It was my first time to own a rare and valuable watch. Just like finding a precious treasure, I wore it on my wrist immediately. My heart was filled with excitement and I was thankful to have my loving father. This watch followed me all around the world through many years of traveling. Even now, it is still working perfectly imprinted with memories of Father.

Father turned around and proudly said to his friend, 'My clumsy son won awards in swimming. He is also a good diver, I taught him well.'

The salesmen and customers joined in the conversation and

praised him for raising his son well. Father felt proud and couldn't hold his smile, I still remembered how happy he was. Father's bragging in front of strangers was quite embarrassing to witness as I stood by his side hoping for it to end. After the watch shop, Father took me to an electronics store hoping to get me a Japanese branded portable cassette radio recorder.

He said, 'Ah Ho, after you arrive in UK, record some cassettes and send them back home.' I nodded to show my promise and asked, 'Father, what gift will you buy for younger sister?'

He whispered, 'She is just a girl, we can just buy her some warm clothes. She doesn't need a brand watch. She is too young and naïve. You take good care of her as the elder brother!' I nodded and we went back home together.

Realizing that I was going to leave Hong Kong shortly, a place I had lived for over a decade, my heart really clenched. As a matter of fact, I was reluctant to leave my home town. Does UK have beautiful beaches? Are there going to be any good martial arts masters? All these thoughts about life in UK, made me more confused and anxious, never in my lifetime had I felt more lost and clueless about what's to come. That same year, I was especially fond of Bruce Lee's movies, especially Fists of Fury. His unbelievable demonstration of martial arts on the TV totally captivated me. I was obsessed with his fast kicks and crazy punches. I was learning Hung Boxing at the time, one of the traditional Chinese Kung Fu originated in Southern China. I also attempted to learn Bruce Lee's famous kick techniques. He developed his own style after much practice. Similarly, after much practice I learnt the different advantages of various martial arts styles, my body sculpted into the ideal body shape with broad shoulders and a defined six pack.

I went swimming whenever I had spare time. I would swim

the full length of the beach, back and forth while I enjoyed the scenery at the golden beach where the shining sand connected with the blue sky at the horizon. The seagulls flapped their wings flying at the line where the water and the sky shared the same color. Swimming in the ocean, I was as free as a fish. Not only did swimming ease my mind, it also aided in building my body strength and health. However, knowing all the new challenges I would have to face in UK, I knew the peace and beautiful scenery were all just momentary.

Eventually, the date to leave Hong Kong arrived – the 8th of July 1973. Carrying the luggage and farewell gifts given by Father, my younger sister and I got ready to leave for the airport. We both dressed up for this special farewell and I even went to the barber shop for a fashionable haircut. Father drove us to the airport. I was waiting at the terminals in Kai Tak International Airport, dreading to say goodbye to relatives and friends. The Kai Tak International Airport used to be located at the heart of Kowloon peninsula, due to the geographical area, it was highly risky and difficult for aircrafts to land. It was eventually demolished in 1998 and was replaced by Chek Lap Kok International Airport in Lantau Island. My good classmates George, Alfred and Lawrence came to bid me farewell. After many years, they have all scattered around the world. George is the only one that I'm still in touch with. George immigrated to Australia not long after I left Hong Kong, he is surely enjoying life overseas. Alfred immigrated to Canada and I met him in the streets of Toronto in Canada. Being apart for so long and living different lifestyles, we no longer have any common topics nor do we share the same passions. After a quick chat, we said goodbye to each other.

Out of all my farewells, Grandma's was undeniably the most

unforgettable one. Even as she said goodbye to her grandchildren, she was strong and unwavering. She was the almighty Hakka elder. My Father showed extreme respect towards grandma and he carefully carried out all the duties bestowed on him as a son-in-law. He kept her updated on her daughter's life in Glasgow and kept her company at all times. Grandma would always just nod and smile. At last, my sister and I headed for boarding. With all the unknowns and the heart wrenching farewells, we started to shed tears. I was worried whether I could ever come back to Hong Kong. What did my future hold? I prayed to God to give me an answer. I kept thinking to myself why I had to leave my father to see my mother, it almost felt like they were a divorced couple. Before I entered the departure terminal, I bid my favorite hometown goodbye. Hong Kong, the place I had lived for more than a decade, good bye. As I welcomed England, please greet us with flowers and not let our paths be filled with disappointments, thistles and thorns.

The airplane that we took was the most advanced one in that year, the Boeing 747. Entering the cabin was just like stepping into a magical world. I used to dream about becoming an aviation engineer, sitting alongside the pilots while we watch the blue sky ahead of us just like a wild eagle soaring across the clouds. We took our seats and tightly buckled our safety belts. This was our first time flying and we would never have imagined our first flight would be to England, ten thousand kilometers away from Hong Kong. Of course, we were naive back then, we saw everything as new and modern. All these experiences were unique and new to us, watching the clouds outside the window, reading the illustrated magazines on the plane, and the first taste of an inflight meal. It was also my first time to see so many foreigners dressed in formal wear, just like gentlemen and ladies in movies. I heard bad things about inflight meals, but after trying one for the first time, I thought it was pleasant enough. Last but not least, it was extraordinary to receive warm services from the air hostess with fine blonde hair. I slowly began to fall asleep as I listened to the music, while heading on our way to London. After a long-distance flight of more than ten hours, the plane finally landed in Heathrow International Airport in London. Father had taught us earlier about how to handle the immigration officer. We had to say we were coming to England for leisure and were visiting our relatives. It was crucial that we should not mention our Mother working in Glasgow as she was working illegally at the time. Just like the immigration officer, Father prepped us prior to the trip.

'What's your name? Where are you going? What's your purpose for coming to the United Kingdom?' He would not stop until I remembered every single word and answer.

After the landing, I was a little bit nervous. I tried to hide my anxiety and stood up straight, holding my sister's hand, we walked towards the immigration desk. We both smiled bright and bubbly, pretending to be in England for fun. It was finally our turn at the customs immigration desk. The female immigration officer with light blonde hair asked, 'Good morning, what's your name?'

I answered immediately, 'Hofer Ho.'

She then looked over to my sister and questioned, 'Who is she?'

I answered confidently, 'She is my sister.'

She said in a friendly surprised tone, 'Really? Your younger sister is so cute!'

She inquired about the reason for our coming to England. Father had predicted all the questions. Remembering all my prepared answers, I had no trouble responding to the officer.

The officer, satisfied with what she heard, smiled and stamped our passports. She said, 'Enjoy the stay!' Hearing the sound of the stamp stomping into our passports gave me a sense of relief. We finally got approved for the visiting visas and passed customs. Like many others, this was the first and last lie ever taught to me by my father, I guess it really worked!

I was so nervous my heart still did not stop pounding after we walked past customs. After the planned strategic questioning, we officially landed in London. That year, I was just seventeen years old, while my sister was twelve. The immigration officer probably thought we were the second generation of a wealthy family from the looks of all our clothes, leather shoes and brand watches as well as our ability to fluently answer all her questions. Without any doubt she approved us for a tourist visa that would last six months.

I looked around excited and curious at the same time with my sister's hand tightly clenched in mine, I carefully followed the airport signs directed to baggage claims. We took two luggage carts and quickly headed to the conveyor belt. We grabbed our luggage fully packed with clothing and gifts and pushed our carts towards customs.

The customs officer firmly asked, 'Do you have cigarettes or wine?'

I confidently answered, 'No'.

After the quick questioning, we were allowed to go. I was still too young then and hated cigarettes and alcohol. Being my ignorant self, I always thought smokers and alcoholics aren't good people. However, as time passed by, I myself became one of those people. I will always remember my first cigarette, it was handed to me by my own Mother in the streets of Glasgow.

We passed through customs smoothly towards the arrival terminal. The arrival hall was packed with people from all around the world. I had never seen so many different ethnicities in one area before, Caucasian, Asian and African. It was definitely my first culture shock. Among the crowd, an unfamiliar voice yelled out my name. The distinctive Cantonese words echoed in my head. I glanced at where the voice was coming from. There stood a small and slim pale Asian male. I didn't recognize him at all, he quickly rushed over to us and introduced himself.

'Hey Cousin! Your mother asked me to pick you up. I'm your Cousin Wai,' he said.

I smiled awkwardly and nodded my head. 'Let's go! I will drive you to see your uncles first!' he said again.

'Okay,' I shyly replied. Like tourists, we followed him closely and passed the crowds of people.

Cousin Wai was my aunt's eldest son. He followed my uncles to England and started his life there at a young age. He married a Scottish woman and they had one son and one daughter. His wife had a full-time job, while his job wasn't as stable. He was interested in public relations. Therefore, he became an agent that primarily worked with Hakka people, helping them purchase and sell properties. He also assisted them through the legal parts of the process. It was a pity that he and my uncles shared one similar hobby; gambling. Just like most Hakka people, they loved the thrills and gains they achieved in casinos. As always, luck cannot always be on their side, they lost a lot of their hard-earned money in their beloved casino halls.

On the way to uncle's house, Cousin Wai babbled about his sufferings and achievements throughout his years in England as he used one hand to hold onto his cigarette while driving at the same time. I watched the roads outside as I listened to him, there were constructions going on and to my surprise all the construction workers were Caucasian. All my life I thought they were the superior race in Hong Kong. Why was there such a big difference between high-class Caucasians in Hong Kong and construction workers in England? As we drove across town, the red double decker buses caught my attention and they were very similar to the ones in Hong Kong. Just like at the construction site, the drivers and passengers were all Caucasian, it was fascinating and strange to see them at different levels in society. Cousin Wai headed onto the highway towards Birmingham and as he sped through the highway, I could see how developed this country was. The detailed road signs flew past us and there were rows of cat's eyes on the road surfaces guiding the vehicles. I was awed by the advanced road structures and development in this country. It was then I was determined to learn how to drive.

After two to three hours, we finally arrived at Birmingham. It was late then, but Cousin Wai surprisingly brought us to a casino! We got out of his car and noticed several Hong Kong young adults were chatting and smoking with some local girls. As we walked toward them, Cousin Wai greeted them in Hakka. He said, 'You two wait for me here, I'm going inside to find your uncle.'

We waited patiently outside the casino, a while later, a familiar face came to greet us. Uncle Shing hugged us and smiled, 'It's very nice you two finally arrived! Your mother is working in Scotland, in the meantime, you two can stay here first. I will take you both to find your other uncle, Uncle Hing, and you two can live at his place.'

'How's your luck tonight?' Cousin Wai interrupted.

'Not too bad,' Uncle Shing struggled.

As we entered the car, one of the Hong Kong young adults called out to Uncle Shing, 'Hey Chef Shing! You want a white girl tonight?'

Uncle Shing didn't answer but smiled. We shuffled into the car and left. Not long after, we arrived at a Chinese take-away shop. It was located in a two-story building. The second floor was a private condo and the first floor was the shop. Once you step into the shop, you were engulfed with the smell of soy sauce and lard, the main ingredients of Chinese cuisine. The first person we saw in the shop was a tiny petite Chinese woman, she was standing behind a large counter at the cash register. Beside her, pinned onto the wall was an enlarged Chinese menu with English translation. The menu included dishes like chicken curry with rice, chicken chop suey with rice and a few popular western dishes like fish and chips. It was strange to me that there were no sitting areas in the shop, it was just one walkway up to the front counter. This was my first time stepping into a Chinese take-away shop in England.

The woman noticed me and gleamed, 'You finally arrived! You must be Ah Ho and she must be Ah Ting!' We responded politely with a small nod, 'Hi, Aunt Hing.'

Uncle Shing and Cousin Wai's Hakka conversation never paused as they chatted in the background. A short moment later, a car parked right in front of the shop. Uncle Hing got out of the car and entered the shop. Once he saw us, he laughed cheerfully and said, 'You guys finally arrived! I just went out for a delivery. Sorry I couldn't make it to the airport! You two can stay with us tonight. We have three bedrooms upstairs.'

They helped us carry the luggage upstairs. Both my sister and I were exhausted, we fell asleep almost immediately after a quick shower. I could faintly hear my relatives chatting away as I slowly drifted off to sleep. Fully rested, I got up early in the morning. I looked out the window and observed my surroundings. The sun was shining down on the town houses nearby, their yards were filled with trees and colorful landscapes. I could hear the birds and small animals playing and singing, one or two tiny birds flying past my window. One by one, adults left their homes and drove away in their vehicles, while children grabbed their bikes and headed off to school with their backpacks. It was a peaceful and wonderful morning for a fresh start. After I brushed my teeth and washed my face, I headed downstairs and saw Uncle Hing. 'Good morning, Ah Ho, what would you like to have for breakfast?' he kindly offered. My stomach rumbled as I quickly replied, 'Anything!'

He laughed, 'Here, you can have some bread. Eat it with some chips and butter, it tastes so good!'

I was skeptical at first, I always have my sandwiches filled with eggs and sausages. Never had I tried one with just potato chips. Maybe this was some kind of English-style breakfast?

Uncle Hing smiled, 'It's very tough to survive in Birmingham. Us, Chinese usually only get to work in restaurants or take-away shops. There aren't any other jobs that are suitable for us.'

Listening to Uncle Hing's experiences, I slowly drank my hot coffee and took my first bite into the sandwich.

Uncle Hing continued his story, 'My wife and I try very hard to maintain this take-away shop. We handle everything small or big. Here, I will show you around so you can help out in the kitchen.'

I quickly swallowed my last few bites of the sandwich and followed him into the kitchen. Right as we entered the kitchen, the big batch of dead chickens on the floor caught my attention.

He said, 'I bought them from the market at an extremely low price. But it comes with a catch, we have to remove the feathers by ourselves.'

Then he picked up the batch of chickens and put them into a huge stock pot. He filled it with hot water to scald them. As he was working with the chickens, he looked at me and said, 'Let's remove the feathers together!'

I tried to stay calm and not show how disgusted I was by the carcasses. I followed my uncle's instructions and removed all the feathers. After taking off the feathers, uncle cut open the chickens and removed the internal organs. Hiding my discomfort, one by one we cleaned and prepped the chickens.

Uncle Hing suddenly laughed and joked, 'Ah Ho, I have a friend who knows your father. He told me your elder uncle smokes opium in Hong Kong. Since your father is a policeman, shouldn't he arrest him?'

I looked at him and stayed silent. Thoughts ran through my mind, I despised his rude and obnoxious friend and him insulting my father. They claimed to be proud Englishmen, living in England, but are they really considered Englishmen, or are they just slaves working for England? My sister and other relatives had all woken up by the time we finished with the chickens. They sat at the table together to enjoy breakfast. Staring at the feathers on the ground and feeling the sweat dripping from my face, I felt like I was in a rural village doing hard labor. Not long after, Uncle Shing arrived to take my sister and I to the train station. In the afternoon, after cleaning myself up and packing our luggage, we left the take-away shop and rushed to the railway station.

After arriving at the train station, we bought our train tickets to Glasgow, Scotland. On the train, we kept quiet as we looked outside at the fast passing scenery. It was still strange for us to see Caucasian people everywhere. We observed them as passengers and they all looked gentle and polite. They were either reading or looking out the window. I couldn't seem to shake the fact that they seemed restrained. My sister curiously looked around like an innocent kid, while I listened with earplugs to my cassette tapes on my brand-new cassette player gifted by my father. I hummed to the tunes sung by the famous Taiwanese singer, Teresa Tang as we stepped one step closer to see our Mother after being apart for months.

Electric Train

Glasgow

We finally arrived in Glasgow, the northern part of Britain. It is the biggest city in Scotland and one of the top three cities in Great Britain. Glasgow is famous for its manufacturing and shipping industries. It has one of the most significant ports in the United Kingdom, making it one of the top ten financial centers in Europe.

We struggled to exit the train as we dragged our heavy luggage with us. The first thing that caught our eyes were the unique walls laid with ancient bricks. As we walked toward the station hall, we noticed the large, tall windows with verdigris frames. The natural and the station's lighting lit up the station. The station was filled with busy passengers rushing to catch their next ride. We were surprised that a lot of them weren't as tall as the Caucasians we had encountered in London, instead most of them were similar in height to me. They wore thick coats paired with formal hats. It seemed to be colder than London.

Dragging the luggage, we stumbled to the exit gate. Standing at the exit was Cousin Ming and Mother. Ah Ting rushed to Mother immediately and hugged her tightly. We hadn't seen her for a long time, we all were excited and happy to finally see each other again. It was a heartwarming reunion.

As a teenage boy I didn't like to express my emotions, perhaps this is because of my introverted nature. I casually greeted my Mother and Cousin Ming. 'How's life?' I asked him.

Central Station

Excitedly he told us all about his experience working at the restaurant and all the struggles he encountered. In Birmingham, Uncle Hing had already told me a bit about the work situation at Mother and Cousin Ming's workplace. I had a clear understanding of their work environment. They worked at a restaurant located in a small town called Motherwell situated right beside Glasgow. My Mother had worked her way up to assistant chef while Cousin Ming was a waiter. They worked six days a week, with weekends being the busiest time of the week. They would often either have Tuesday or Wednesday off. The tough labor work in the kitchen had made my Mother's hands coarse and stronger. Compared to the past she seemed to have gotten paler and gained some weight. Knowing my mother's personality, I knew she would not be an assistant chef for long. She was there to gain and master the skills to prepare dishes and soon she would be off to start her own business.

In the United Kingdom, typical Chinese restaurants and take-away shops are often family businesses. Many Hakka people took the opportunity to immigrate to the United Kingdom and start their own small family businesses. It was a whole new world for them. With a relatively simple operating system, typically take-away shops would have one chef, also known as the 'wok master' handling the majority of the cooking, while the assistant would be responsible for deep-fried dishes such as fish and chips, sweet and sour pork and so on. The chef would also manage the food supply and preparation. During rush hour, the chef would step in to help grill fillet steak and pork chop. Mother and Cousin Ming seemed to be very satisfied with working at the restaurant but complained about the intensive labor. No doubt, they earned more money than in Hong Kong, but despite saying they were happy with where they worked, we could tell they felt conflicted. Listening to their stories, I started to think back to my simple and carefree life in Hong Kong. I started to blame my Mother for asking me to come to Scotland.

'Mom! Why did you choose to come to Scotland? How do you even know this is a good place for us?' I aggressively questioned.

She bellowed, 'I have traveled so far for your future. If we just stayed in Hong Kong, there was no way we could afford to send you to university! I earn more money here! You can ask your Cousin Ming too!' I could tell I'd upset her. Cousin Ming nodded awkwardly and agreed with her.

I didn't know if she was right or wrong, but I held on to my suspicions. We were quiet after that as we walked towards the taxi lineup. We all silently entered the taxi and left the railway station. We arrived at Uncle Hon's house where Mother had arranged for us to stay. After some short greetings, Mother and Cousin Ming left to return to work in Motherwell. We were left alone at Uncle Hon's house.

Uncle Hon lived at the east side of the city on Hill Street. It was surrounded by ancient buildings, all over a hundred years old and had six to seven floors with the majority of them built with dark gray brick. Uncle lived in one of these apartments on the fourth floor. The building wasn't equipped with an elevator so we slowly dragged our luggage up the four flights of stairs.

Hill Street

During our stay, Uncle Hon was away in New York, working for a restaurant. We were taken care of by his wife, born in Sha

Tau Kok, New Territories in Hong Kong; this was Uncle Hon's second marriage. Like us, she is Hakka and very ordinary except her tendency to chat. Similar to my Mother's personality, she was fond of criticizing others' flaws. It was very difficult to get along with her. I questioned why Mother would arrange for us to stay with her. We mostly kept to ourselves and listened to her complaints and rants. The neighbors were also from Hong Kong. To no one's surprise they were also Hakka people from Yuen Long, New Territories in Hong Kong. Like many Hakka people, they worked in a restaurant. They have a son named Ah Kong, similar age as me. During our stay, they did us a favor by helping us with our application process to our neighborhood high school. We became close friends with Ah Kong. Little did I know; Ah Kong would eventually become my brother-in-law.

During our school application process, my mother, Cousin Ming and Auntie did nothing to help us. I constantly debated the real purpose of my stay. Compared to Hong Kong, Scotland was cold and damp, the sky was constantly dark and dull. I started to feel moody and depressed, this was not the place I would like to study in. Ever since I had arrived, I had known this was not a place I could find the joy to enjoy my teenage life, to fall in love, study or mature in. I had recurring thoughts of buying a plane ticket and leave Scotland. I could live with my Father in Hong Kong. I missed my high school classmates, my life in Stanley, my freedom. Why was I forced to leave my perfect life and sent to an unknown place to suffer so far away from home? As Mother and Cousin Ming had to work most of the week, our neighbor Ah Kong was the only one to take us to see the school's principal. At the principal's office, he looked over our paperwork and looked me into the eye.

'Hofer, you're already seventeen. It would be more beneficial for you to find work. Your sister is still young so she can continue her studies,' he spoke with a very deep Scottish accent.

It was very hard to understand at first. I didn't answer him right away, I only had one thought in my mind; I am doomed, he is not going to enroll me. Despite my worries, he eventually started to arrange our school admission. To our surprise he didn't question our immigration status. Perhaps, he forgot to ask us, or he simply didn't care. I was just pleased and excited to find out the tuition was free at the local high school. My top priority was to get us back into school as soon as possible. In the following months, Ah Kong and I went to school. There were only a few Chinese students enrolled there. Trying to stick to our comfort zones, we all gathered around noon to enjoy our lunches. I didn't enjoy the lunch there much and it never came with rice. The most common dish was fish and chips. After school, I headed down with my newfound friends to Sauchiehall Street. We would walk down the hill while chatting and window-shopping. We were often left alone at home. Most days we would cook our own meals. Auntie showed up on Mondays or Tuesday mornings. At night when she returned from work, she would blast famous Taiwanese songs. Her favorite singer is Teresa Tang, I can still remember the lyrics of 'The Story of a Small Town' or 'The Moon Represents My Heart'. I know these songs so fluently I can recite them backwards. On work days, Auntie came back home at two or three in the morning. Like my Mother, she was a tough hard-working woman.

I could not recall when Ah Mo arrived in Glasgow, all I remembered was knowing my Father was left all alone in Hong Kong, I figured with his growing loneliness he would eventually find a mistress to keep him company him. Uncle Hon eventually came back from the United States. We all went out for afternoon tea on my Mother and Cousin Ming's day off. We went to a dim sum restaurant called Far East Cantonese Restaurant. Uncle Hon talked about his experiences in New York and claimed he would never go back since he didn't get the green card. We later heard a rumor that he was trying to avoid an American Chinese lady that was madly obsessed with him. Knowing he made more money in America, Auntie complained about his decision to not return to New York. Drowning out the illogical and disruptive conversations, all three of us just sat quietly enjoying our delicious dim sum. As our stay extended, Uncle Hon and his wife's attitude towards us shifted. They slowly started to nitpick our small behaviors. I wondered if my mother had paid rent for our stay and if this was the reason behind the attitude change. We felt quite hopeless with the constant nagging. Knowing our mother, she wouldn't listen to our discontent, we knew to just keep quiet and endure. Mother and Cousin Ming left to work in Motherwell. On the rare occasion we were in the same room, they never asked about our studies or how we were doing. As a Mother, she knew nothing about our problems in life or school. She didn't seem to care about our feelings at all. Compared to Hong Kong, the curriculum at our public high school was not advanced, as a result, our grades in science and math surpassed other local students. For not long after, I was transferred to another school enrolled in O level courses to prepare for university.

One day, the principal saw me and told me, 'Hofer, I did not expect you to achieve such high grades. I was wrong about you. I am sure you will enter a wonderful university and have a bright future. Good luck!'

I smiled and shook his hand as he was leaving. I was overjoyed and proud of myself.

One stormy night, Ah Mo didn't think before he spoke and offended Uncle Hon. They burst into an aggressive argument that started with dinner leftovers. It quickly escalated to personal attacks and hostile comments. I clearly remember the harsh words that came out of my Uncle's mouth.

'Your stupid mother is so naive! Sending you all here, you will be better off marrying a Scottish girl and being a waiter forever! Just get a job, grow old and die! You all want to be university graduates? What a fucking joke! Stop daydreaming!' He yelled as he pointed his fingers at us.

I was furious but I held in my anger. You wait and see! I was determined to graduate from university and rise up in life. I would make my mother and family proud!

After the fierce quarrel, Uncle Hon and Auntie ordered us to leave their house immediately. With nowhere to go, we headed to bed and sobbed in silence. Knowing we were about to get kicked out soon, I couldn't fall asleep at all. I blamed my mother for bringing us here, our lives would've been more peaceful in Hong Kong. We would not be living in someone's place behaving carefully at all times if we stayed in Hong Kong. I hated Uncle and Auntie's actions, despite our silence and obedience, they decided to kick us out without any mercy. Now, we were homeless and had no say at all.

The following day, I skipped school and went to see Ah Kong. I told him to call my mother and tell her what had happened. We quickly scrambled to search for a place to stay. Soon we found a one-bedroom apartment nearby to rent. The three of us packed our luggage quickly and prepared to tow our heavy iron beds to the apartment. Withholding our tears, the three of us dragged our beds and belongings step by step down four flights of stairs. The training in Hung Boxing didn't go to waste as I carried down the heavy loads. The iron beds felt like mountains pressing down on my cold shoulders. After a full day of labor, we were all exhausted and sound asleep. When we woke up, we were surprised by the amount of snow outside our apartment. It had turned the whole city into a winter wonderland covered by thick fluffy snow. I could feel the breeze leaking in from the windowsills. Despite the temperature, I could feel my anger burning fiercely. Being kicked out by our bloody relative during the middle of winter made me realize how weak our family connection was. Since that day I have never seen Uncle Hon or Auntie's family again.

Hardships are inevitable in life and it is through these hardships where we learn to adapt and become tougher and stronger. These challenges helped me generate motivation and devotion to achieve my goals. I knew I would have more slopes to overcome in my lifetime. I told myself to overcome this incident and always focus on the paths ahead.

Without any paths behind me, I could only focus to move ahead. The sharp edge of a sword comes from sharpening. Although the process was painful, the constant verbal abuse and coldhearted comments from Uncle Hon and his wife greatly fueled our ambitions. As a result of their inspiration, each of us is not only a university graduate but has gone on to achieve Masters and PhDs.

We soon appointed a lawyer in Scotland to assist us in applying for student visas. We were all glad to hear good news from the lawyer; all our visas were granted with work permits. We all thought this was the end of our misery and we could finally settle down and concentrate on our studies. Unfortunately for us, this peace did not last long, Mother's strong desire for money eventually destroyed our short moment of joy and changed our lives again. I don't know whose idea it was, but Mother and Cousin Ming decided to fulfill their ambitions and started to look for a shop of their own. They spent days looking at spaces to purchase for their Chinese take-away shop. Finally, they found an old take-away shop for sale. Being the eldest son, I knew there were legal responsibilities linked to having your own business. I asked them to discuss the application for a permanent right of abode from the British Government with our lawyer, in hopes of staying in Glasgow and opening our own shop. Naturally, we were included with the application. However due to ignorance and greed, the results ultimately brought more misfortune to our family.

Glasgow City

During the wait for the resident visa, Mother started to grow impatient. Despite knowing it is illegal to open a shop without a visa, Mother ignored it and started her business. Like the shop she worked in before, she opened a traditional Hakka style fast food take-away shop. I was constantly doubting my mother's true purpose for coming to Britain, she claimed it was for our studies, but in reality, she probably wanted to make a big fortune. Perhaps, she was trying to do both at the same time. There was little in her mind other than making money. Probably, greed fueled her ignorance and she had completely forgotten the fact that she left her husband alone in Hong Kong. Being bystanders was mentally and physically challenging. We were all very tired of the lifestyle our mother exposed us to. We were her cheap labor in assembling her shop. The constant physical strength could be restored through a good night rest, but our mental state was slowly deteriorating. Growing up in the traditional Hakka family, we knew our mother was bound to traditional ways of training her children. We were always expected to do anything our elders ordered us to do, but as the younger generation, did we really have to obey every demand? I started to question our traditional Confucius ways. Is it really correct? The core beliefs of Confucianism include kindness, righteousness, wisdom, trust, loyalty and of course the most important one, filial piety. Perhaps, Confucius or Mencius' ways of teaching was the way emperors maintained and protected their dominant authoritarianism.

Drumchapel

Chinese Food Take-away Shop in Drumchapel Road

It seemed like Mother's destiny when she luckily purchased a Chinese food take-away shop for around five thousand pounds. It would almost cost her half a million dollars if purchased today. In order to gather funds for the shop, she asked Father for financial assistance. She never told me how much she received, but it was enough to cover the costs. Cousin Ming and Mother became business partners and their own bosses. This new shop located in Drumchapel was their dream and their escape from the working class. After they purchased the shop, Mother and Cousin Ming returned to Hill Street to live with us. We would all travel by bus to the shop, it usually took us about thirty minutes. Ah Mo, Ah Ting and I would go to the school in the morning and help out at the shop after school. Since Ah Ting was still quite young then, she was assigned the simple chores. We would work until the shop closed at eleven or twelve o'clock late at night. We really grew to experience how it was like to work and study at the same time. The only difference was our boss was also our strict and tough mother. Instead of regular hourly pay, she gave us fifty pounds per week with free meals and accommodation.

Prior to coming to Scotland, I hated smoking. However, as Mother started to smoke, she decided to offer me my first cigarette. The weather in Glasgow was constantly humid and cold, it was easy to lack the motivation to wake up at six o'clock in the morning. Not only that, we had to work until midnight every night. I reluctantly grabbed the cigarette my mother offered me and not long after, it was my morning routine to have a smoke and drink strong coffee. One of the perks working at the shop was free cigarettes. After many years of smoking, Dunhill is by far my favorite.

Life started to become a regular routine. Every day we would go to school then to work. We didn't have anywhere else to visit. The shop was forty-five minutes away from the city. It was surrounded by low-income public housing, mostly occupied by local workers. The shop was located in a small shopping center on Drumchapel Road. We shared this small shopping center with a barber shop, fish and chips shop, a small supermarket and a gas station. A famous Scottish writer, Mrs. Mary Backie once described Drumchapel and the local residents in her interview,

'I remember a time where you could walk out and talk to your neighbors, leave your doors wide open. You can leave the keys in the door and ask people to come in for a cup of tea. You can't do that now, you can't get your doors locked quick enough.'

Work at the Take-away Shop in Drumchapel

During busy weekends, we would blast music at the shop to make it more bearable. We would listen to pop songs by famous English singers like Rod Stewart or Cliff Richard. My favorite songs are definitely 'I Am Sailing' and 'Bachelor Boy'. I would picture myself sailing across the wide ocean adventuring into the unknown. Listening to their songs always cheered me up. There would be times when customers sang along with their drunk friends after a few drinks. They loved singing along to 'Five Hundred Miles' and 'Country Roads Take Me Home'. It's always entertaining to watch these rowdy customers, although occasionally these funny moments would turn into aggressive fights.

Recalling all the fights between our parents, regular customer disputes weren't shocking to us. Sometimes, I enjoyed watching fights that I did not have to pay for. It usually ended up with us calling the police to clean up the messy situation. With all the constant visits, the sergeant eventually became our regular customer and friend. Having a father in the police force, we had a sense of familiarity with the police force. The sergeant always came in for regular meals and whenever we called him to stop fights, he would always arrive within minutes. They were truly efficient!

There was one very memorable fight that occurred on the weekend at midnight. We were fully occupied inside the shop that night, with customers waiting for orders. Our customers were enjoying their meals, singing and dancing along to the songs when suddenly, a taxi driver threw a punch at the glass door and shattered it. He began to throw punches at customers, most fought back while some were injured with blood on their faces. Without any hesitation, I ran to the kitchen and grabbed the biggest cleaver I could find. I held it tight standing behind the front counter. Luckily for us, the counter was extremely high, to avoid burglars and offer protection for staff. Ah Ting, rushed to the kitchen's phone and called the police. We watched the fight while hiding behind the front counter. It lasted for around ten minutes and it was strange that there was no attempt to enter the kitchen or the cash register. The battleground was filled with unconscious and bloody men, screaming women and food scattered all over the walls and floors.

Finally, the police cars arrived, one after another. The men gradually stopped fighting as they saw the policemen enter the shop. We were all shaking in fear hiding in the kitchen, and didn't dare to make any sound. We could hear yelling, screams and people crying. We peaked outside and saw five or six policemen holding batons against the kneeling men. The wounded were lying on the ground with bleeding cuts on their faces. Not long after, we heard the ambulance rushing towards the shop. The medics rushed in and started to treat the wounded in the shop.

After getting the situation under control, the police sergeant came to us with a very serious expression.

He said, 'The fight this time is very serious. Bloody hell! We will need you to come back to the police station as witnesses.'

Cousin Ming and I nodded and followed them to the police station. Mother, Ah Ting, and Ah Mo stayed behind to clean up the scene. It was a miracle we didn't get injured in the middle of this fight and we were so glad to know everyone just had minor injuries. Besides the rowdy fights, this shop also had its shining moments. Our mother being a full-time housewife, came alone to Britain to learn cooking. She started from washing dishes and worked her way up to becoming head chef. The woks made in England are not light, different from the traditional Chinese wok, they are manufactured with a wooden stick connected to an iron pan. You need to use your left hand to pull forward and backwards, while you use your right hand to hold the spatula to keep stirring the food. It almost looks like you are practicing Wing Chun. The heat of the stove is so fierce, you could finish cooking a dish within a minute. Mother gradually taught her cooking techniques to Cousin Ming and I.

After a few months, Cousin Ming's father, our Uncle Shing came to join us from Birmingham. He started to work at our shop as a chef, specialising in slicing pork and cooking beef steaks. Every week he would make curry paste, filled with twenty bags of flour, curry powder, pepper and all sorts of spices. It took hours to make and would last up to two weeks. We would add water to turn it into delicious curry sauce. His curry sauce was our most popular dish, including curry chicken, curry beef and curry pork. Business was starting to pick up after a few more months and Mother decided to purchase a second-hand wagon to make it more convenient for us to purchase groceries for the shop. Mother had really shown her leadership skills through her success with starting the food business. She had grown from being a rural girl to a housewife and eventually her own boss owning her first take-away shop.

For big packages of groceries, we split them between all of us to get them prepped. Like professional factories, we would then arrange the foodstuff one by one down the assembly line. Since weekends were the busiest, every Friday we would come to the shop after class to help prep for the weekend. Almost all our food and take-away boxes were pre-prepared in the kitchen. Ah Mo would take orders from customers at the counter, while Ah Ting will coordinate between the front and the back. She would notify the kitchen of new orders and I started prepping the order. I would help out with the simple jobs like frying the rice or making curry sauce. Sometimes, I would be at the front counter receiving orders. Most days, I had to remember more than ten orders and pack them quickly and efficiently. The take-out boxes were made out of aluminum with a cardboard lid and one shiny foil side to keep the heat in. I used my fingertips to press into the aluminum folds to avoid the food from spilling. On busy nights, I pressed over a hundred boxes. The sharp aluminum folds would scratch my fingers and by the end of the night, my fingertips would be bleeding. Day after day, I had to constantly wrap them in bandages.

Our weekends were all spent on involuntary work, sometimes I forgot I was a foreign student. To reward us for our hard work, Mother would grill us a giant fillet steak every Saturday. It filled us right up just in time for bed. Of course, to go along with the steak, we enjoyed cigarettes and alcohol. I started to learn how to enjoy beer and whiskey. Having one or two cups a day helped me fall asleep faster. Every morning, as soon as I opened my eyes, I could feel the pain lingering in my fingers. My right arm had become stronger after repeatedly cooking with the wok.

Drumchapel Train Station

No matter how straining the work at the shop, we still had to get up every morning to go to school. At school people commented on my dark eyes, I looked like a student who never got enough sleep. One day, while daydreaming in class, our math teacher asked me to answer the question on the board. Surprised, I stood up not knowing where I was for a second. I quickly stared at the white board and after a few seconds, I managed to give the right answer.

'Hofer, is there a reason why you always look so tired?' she asked kindly.

I explained I was tired from working at my mother's take-away shop. She looked sympathetic and joked, 'Oh, that doesn't matter. You can come to my class and take a nap again.' Everyone in class burst into laughter. Knowing she was just joking, I grinned a little and sat back down. Math class was extremely easy for me. To my surprise, I achieved the 0 level all-subject champion. The school, in return, rewarded me with fifty pounds. I really enjoyed my studies at Clydebank Technical College.

Clydebank Technical College

Knowing I wanted to pursue higher education, I started to prepare for my university entrance examination. After so many months, we were still waiting for our abode's right approval from the British Government. It felt like forever waiting for them to complete the application. Since we never got the approval or any notice from the lawyer, we continued to live our daily lives like locals. Many Scottish teenagers would come by our shop to buy take-away. A lot of young teenage girls started to pay attention to me. Every now and then, these girls would also flirt with Cousin Ming. He would take days off to drive around Glasgow with them. Sometimes, I would join in on their rides. We were always cautious not to mention anything at the shop knowing my mother would be furious if she found out.

One day, I came across a short, slim and pretty Scottish girl. She always came in to buy food with her friends. She started coming in once a week, eventually she started to come every day. She didn't have very much money since she would only buy the plain curry sauce with rice or chips. After a while, I could not help myself but finally asked her, 'Do you like Chinese food that much, to come every day?' She smiled and nodded, 'Yes! I love Chinese food! Especially your curry.' She spoke in a very heavy Scottish accent. After that encounter we started to talk every day. We chatted about everything and my English slowly started to bear resemblance to the Scottish accent. Not long after, we began to date secretly. She was my first lovely girlfriend. Perhaps, I finally felt I love for Glasgow because of our puppy love. Our relationship was sweet but lasted short. Mother had eventually discovered our relationship and started to give her bad attitude whenever she came by to visit. Under the pressure of my mother and Uncle Hon's past experiences with his Caucasian ex-wife, I decided to end our relationship early to spare us pain in the future.

I decided to focus mainly on my studies. During that time, Ah Kong came to see Ah Ting frequently and of course my Mother was not very pleased with the visits. She knew he wasn't a good student and would not suit her daughter. Ah Mo was also secretly dating a new immigrant from Hong Kong, he kept it away from the family drama, but that relationship didn't last long either.

On a regular evening when there weren't many customers, Ah Mo and Ah Ting were home preparing for their exam. I stayed at the shop to help out. All of a sudden, Mother moaned in pain, she clenched her stomach with sweat dripping down her face. We all thought it might be just a regular stomachache, however the symptoms weren't fading. After a several hours, Cousin Ming decided to drive her to the hospital. Uncle and I stayed at the shop to serve our customers till midnight. They found out it was acute appendicitis; Mother had no choice but to have an operation immediately. With Mother sick and unable to work, Uncle asked me if I would want to work or if they should close the shop until her full recovery. In the end, it was decided to have me work during my exam preparation time. Throughout the next few weeks, I had to study and work long hours every day. Not being able to focus on my studies hindered my exam results. After one month, Mother recovered and our examinations came to an end. Soon after it was time for me to prepare for my university entrance exam. I had two career dreams in mind, one was aircraft engineering and the other was pharmacy. I decided to apply for both. Mother always liked to keep herself busy, she refused to stay home and rest. During her recovery stage, she would come to the shop and monitor our work. At the beginning, she did light jobs and passed on the cooking to Uncle Shing, Cousin Ming and I. It was that month where I developed my cooking skills. I would even show off to customers, flipping ingredients in the air with the wok. I was very pleased to hear applause from my audience.

After a long wait, we finally heard from our lawyer, he informed us that the Immigration Office would like to check on our business finance and tax situation. Not knowing the importance of this request, Mother lied to the Tax Bureau stating she didn't earn much money from her business. However, the fact was Mother's business profits were enough to purchase a house in Glasgow. Due to this dishonesty, the Government rejected the right of abode application a few months later. While devastated, the lawyer assured us that we could appeal the results and stay in Scotland for another year or two. That was not the only misfortune we had that month. I learned that my examination results were not high enough to enter either university. My dreams were instantly shattered. I knew I had to choose either to study again or to apply at a science and technology institution. In the end, with less options, I applied to Huddersfield Polytechnic of Northern England to study biochemistry.

Huddersfield was five to six hours away from Glasgow. To make traveling more convenient, I left home and started to live alone. Every weekend, I took the train back to Glasgow to help out at the shop. I felt great to be alone and free, I would observe the others around me and listen to their stories. I gradually became introverted and enjoyed my solitude.

This independent life had allowed me to meet more local citizens, immigrants and international students. During those years of my life, I didn't talk in Cantonese, most days it would be either English or Hakka dialect. Disappointed with my attempt to enter pharmacy, I tried again to apply for another university for the coming year. At the same time, I was constantly praying that our lawyer could help us stay longer so I could accomplish my studies in Britain.

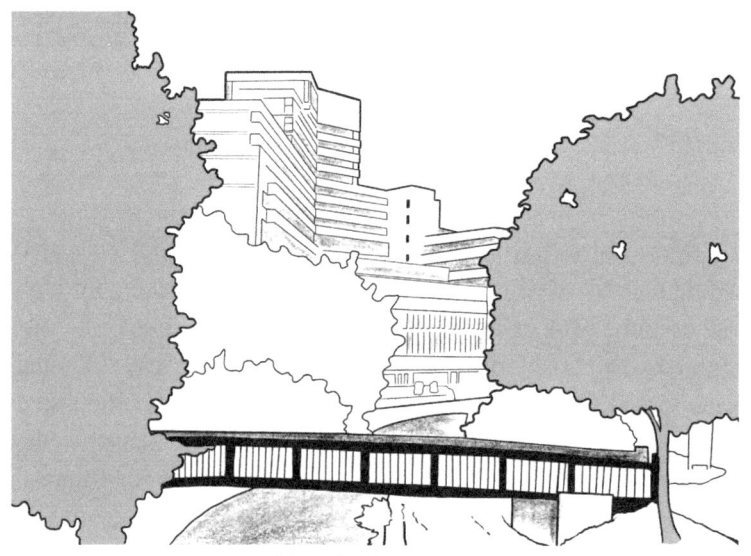
Huddersfield Polytechnic

After months of waiting, the appeal was denied; I had just finished my freshman year at college. I was also accepted to study pharmacy as a first-year student in a nearby university. Ah Ting had passed her university entrance exam. Ah Mo, predictably failed his courses and had to retake his preparatory courses. Since the appeal failed, we were ordered to leave the country immediately. Everything had to be stopped, including our schooling. We had no idea what to do with our shop. Not knowing what was in store for us in the future, we were lost and confused. We couldn't accept the outcome of our hard work. We were mad at the government and the way they treated their colony's citizens.

Game Over

We were not left with many choices, especially not ones that would help us stay in Scotland. Without clearly thinking through our options, Mother decided to take the riskiest route. She just ignored the order of Immigration Office to leave United Kingdom and continued to stay in Scotland illegally. She asked Ah Ting to stay with her to continue her studies in Glasgow. She also asked me to apply to Ah Ching's university in Canada, Windsor University. Cousin Ming and Ah Mo followed suit and applied to study in Canada as well. Uncle Shing had his right of abode in the United Kingdom so he continued to work at the shop. He also applied for a family visa for his wife and two daughters, Six Mei and Little Mei, in Hong Kong to join them in Scotland. Ironically, his elder son, Cousin Ming didn't qualify to stay in UK because he was treated as an adult being over twenty-one. Mother, no longer able to work at her own shop, left to work at a restaurant in a nearby town to continue earning her favorite pounds.

Before I left, I asked Mother why she refused to go back to Hong Kong. Her answer was quite simple. She said, 'Son, it is easier to earn money here. I will do my best to keep earning money, nothing will ever stop me!' She seemed to have forgotten about her husband in Hong Kong.

I was the first person to leave Glasgow. I flew to Paris and planned to stay in France for a while. Simultaneously, Ah Ching, my elder sister started to help me with my application to Windsor University. While I waited for the result of my application, I wandered Paris as a tourist. In Paris, I rented a small room in the loft, typically reserved for maids and servants, for temporary shelter. It was affordable and enough for a short stay. Both the toilet and bathroom were shared amongst different tenants. I could not afford to waste any time. I started my mornings with learning French at Alliance Francaise and wandered the streets in the afternoon. McDonalds had become my main food source to save on money. Sometimes, I bought croissants and drinks to enjoy in my small room. I loved the different styles of croissants but I barely had rice while I stayed in Paris. I would have been daydreaming to have Chinese cuisines in Paris which were really expensive. Despite Paris being one of the most romantic and culturally flourished destinations, I was in no mood to immerse myself into my surroundings. All I could think of was my university application and my mother's shop. After a simple dinner, I would walk along Seine, passing by the most iconic Parisian attractions; the Notre Dame de Paris, Paris' symbol- Eiffel Tower and the Louvre Museum. Paris is really a city full of historical, cultural and artistic presence.

Under dimly lit street lamps, intimate couples enjoyed their night together surrounded by city night lights in the romantic atmosphere. As I watched them, loneliness slowly crept in. Tired from walking, I went to a nearby burger joint to have dinner. Just like that my days in Paris flew by. I always believe that in life, your luck has its expiration day. No matter good or bad, eventually it will run out. Finally, after three months of waiting in Paris, I received my acceptance letter from Windsor University. I hurried to the Canadian consulate in Paris and applied for a student visa. That was the moment I realized my bad luck was about to end. Everything seemed to go smoothly. My visa was approved within the hour and I walked out of the consulate feeling relieved. The heavy load on my chest had finally been lifted. Immediately after, I called Mother to tell her my good news. To my surprise, she was proud and happy to hear what I had accomplished.

She cried and said, 'That's great news son! Now your brother and Cousin Ming can follow your steps.'

I paused and thought, wouldn't it be best if Mother returned to Hong Kong and reunited with Father since most of us would be studying in Canada? However, knowing Mother's personality, I decided not to question her again. She had always been the only one that would decide what was best for her. She would not listen to anyone's suggestions or opinions. After a short talk we hung up. That night, I wondered, perhaps Mother had a new boyfriend in Scotland. I still didn't understand why she was willing to stay in Scotland as an illegal worker rather than returning home to her husband. She would not have to suffer as much if she returned to Hong Kong. Ah Mo, Cousin Ming and I all eventually went to Canada one after another. I wouldn't waste any time in Canada because I knew my studies were already delayed. The chance to study in Canada was the turning point of my life. Soon after, Uncle Shing's family got approval from the British Government and settled down in Glasgow. They took over Mother's shop and continued the business. Ah Ting continued her studies in Glasgow and helped out at the shop during her vacations. Oddly, no one suspected Mother and Ah Ting's status and they continued their lives as usual. They continued to live in Glasgow for the next few years. I was amazed by my Mother's fearlessness and her sacrifices. Eventually, after two and a half years of studying, I smoothly graduated and received my first degree in Canada. I then moved on and continued my honorary degree courses. I even planned to achieve a masters. In the time I stayed in Canada, I spent time living with Ah Ching. Just like her mother, she was born with the ambition to earn money. Despite not having a work permit, she worked illegally at a local restaurant. She would spend more time working than at school. It was never clear if she ever finished her university degree.

Time quickly passed by with everyone concentrating on their own lives. After three years, we heard bad news from Scotland. On the day of Ah Ting's last graduation exam, two immigration officers were waiting for her at the school's gate. They told her, a woman with a strong Chinese accent reported her case to Home Office. Both her and Mother's names were provided to the officers, including her university address. In fact, the officers arrived earlier in the day and spoke to the principal. The principal was fully aware of the consequences if he let them see Ah Ting before her exam ended. He tried his best to sway them from interrupting her examinations by telling them her excellent achievements and never having any outstanding college fees. He successfully persuaded them to arrest her after her exams. This was definitely a small glimmer of hope amid all the misfortune. Ah Ting was arrested and quietly sat inside the police car. With tears in her eyes, she was interrogated by the police. The policeman drove around the streets while asking Ah Ting where her mother was. He asked her information about her family members and where they lived. Ah Ting stayed quiet with her head down, at the age of eighteen, she was fully aware of her right to remain silent. After circling around all the places, they knew, the police had no choice but to lock her up in the detention center. The detention guard took a look at Ah Ting and felt sympathetic towards her situation. He kindly placed her in an independent detention center with less restrictions. That night, she couldn't sleep, tears were running down her cheeks as she sobbed through the night. She tried to clear her thoughts and gradually calmed down. She thought the worst-case scenario is deportation back to Hong Kong and she realized maybe it was not as bad as she thought it was. After calming down she patiently waited in her cell.

Ah Ching rushed all the way from Canada to help Mother.

In the morning, a few days later, Mother rushed into the detention center with Ah Ching. Ah Ting was furious when she saw Mother there.

'Mom! What the hell are you doing here? Are you crazy? Don't you know they are looking for you? Leave right now! They won't lock me up forever, we will meet in Hong Kong,' she whispered at Mother but she didn't waiver.

'I am not a coward, if they dare, let them come and catch me!' Mother said proudly.

'This is not a joke! Leave! I don't want us both to be in jail, just leave,' Ah Ting was almost in tears trying to persuade her to go.

Mother had lived in Britain closed to a decade and she had a lot of things to handle before she could be arrested. She went to withdraw all her money at the bank and ensured it is safe and secure. Other matters were less important to her.

In less than three days, Mother's restaurant was surrounded by police and immigration officers. Mother still tried to resist the arrest, she held a shovel as a weapon and was prepared to fight them. She caused injuries to two policewomen during the arrest and in return the police retaliated and Mother was beaten down by two policemen. She was thrown into the police wagon with handcuffs. She was charged with assault of police officers, resisting arrest and illegally working with no valid permit. With so many charges made that night, Mother was put into jail for her crimes.

Imprisonment

Everyone has to pay the price for what they've done. Mother was no exception, however in the process of enduring the consequences she dragged Ah Ting with her as they waited in jail for the court sentence. There were many cells inside the prison, including all types of criminals, murderers, thieves and rapists. Mother was emotionally unstable after her arrest and constantly threw tantrums. Almost every day, she yelled and screamed and some would've thought she was insane. The prison guards didn't understand what she was yelling about, so Ah Ting was stuck with the role as her translator. The daily routines inside a prison were predetermined, exercise in the morning, lots of cleaning duties and free time after. They were offered three meals daily. Mother was so bold, she started to challenge the prison guards and refused to be cooperative.

She didn't do the assigned work and yelled at the guards, 'I am a prisoner, I am not your janitor to clean fucking toilets.'

No doubt, she was there to be locked up not to clean toilets. The guards warned her not to make any more trouble, but Mother just ignored them and continued her rant. Mother was self-centered and didn't care about anything else. To further exaggerate her dissatisfaction, she threatened the guards by attempting to commit suicide. Perhaps, losing her dream and the shop did make her insane.

The Days in the Jail

As a result, Mother was put into a strait jacket, her hands and feet were tied up and she was put into an extremely small isolated chamber filled with thick padded walls. The guards claimed whosoever enters that chamber would calm down promptly and obey. She was locked up in there for hours. Witnessing all this her youngest daughter couldn't help but shed more tears, she was furious and disappointed by her mother's actions.

Several days later, they were moved to an independent cell with stricter security before the court's announcement. Ah Ching was busy searching for a lawyer, in hopes of removing any criminal charges placed on Mother or Ah Ting.

It was a surprise that Ah Ting held it together in the cell. She became calm and mature after her unfortunate stay in jail. When Ah Kong, her boyfriend and childhood friend came to visit her, he became the weak one and burst into tears. It was from then on, their relationship grew stronger and more stable.

What was shocking to us was Uncle Shing's family didn't

visit the prison. They didn't seem to care about their relative's imprisonment. Ah Ting later revealed that there were arguments between Mother and Uncle Shing's daughters, Six Mei and Little Mei, a few days before the immigration officers visited Ah Ting's college. Thinking back to the timing of their arrest, it seemed highly possible that Uncle Shing's family might have been the ones that reported their illegal status.

We suspected that Six Mei, Little Mei or both had betrayed our family and ratted us out to the Home Office in order to solely take over Mother's shop. However, Mother insisted Ah Kong, Ah Ting's boyfriend, was the informant. She accused him without any proof, but in hopes that blaming him would help end her daughter's relationship and shift any hatred towards him. Nevertheless, I really hope one day this riddle will be untied and God would give the final verdict before we die!

After a full month of imprisonment, their court sentences finally arrived. The benevolent judge praised Mother's great love for her family and her willingness to take risks to stay in UK illegally for her children's education. The judge criticized Home Office for the long delay in handling our appeal and right to abode application for our family that became a tragedy indeed. The criminal charges for assaulting police officers had been withdrawn. We were so glad and relieved with the results and thanked our lawyer for a successful defense.

After all the court duties were done, Mother and Ah Ting were immediately deported. Under the accompaniment of two immigration officers, they were escorted on the flight back to Hong Kong. Their long-expired passports had been handed over to the flight attendant for safekeeping until the plane took off. In the end, Mother and her youngest daughter were forced back to her original home, Hong Kong. Her eldest daughter, Ah Ching accomplished rescuing her Mother and sister and flew back to Canada. I picked her up at Toronto airport. She cried like hell and talked endlessly.

Perhaps, beauty is hidden in the difficulties and sufferings of everyday life, however Mother did not see the beauty that came out of her long journey to UK. Ah Ting on the other hand, had experienced so much, her personality changed. She matured into a strong and independent Hakka woman in little over a month. Mother's dream in Britain had officially ended. Not only that, little did Mother know, she was about to return to a different era of Hong Kong. Hong Kong was about to enter into 1997 and the British Government had once again started offering Hong Kong citizens the right of abode in Britain. Irony struck our family when Father was accepted as one of those granted the right to live in Britain. Perhaps, this was her karma for leaving her husband all alone because of her strong and overbearing character.

After finishing her studies in Canada, Ah Ching met her soon to be husband and moved to Chicago, USA. Their marriage granted her citizenship in the United States and she enjoyed her free democratic life with her American born Chinese husband. I, on the other hand, decided to return to Hong Kong from Canada and start my life there. I had deep roots in Hong Kong and I feel obligated to protect the dignity of Hong Kong people. I truly believed my chance to shine was back in my home town. Being affected by my childhood role model, Bruce Lee, I wanted to follow his morals to become a sincere and honest man even under the pressure of authorities and money. To follow this dream, I chose to develop my career in Hong Kong for long term.

After my return, memories of Glasgow slowly started to fade away. I still miss the taste of their whiskey and my passionate Scottish friends and classmates. I have occasionally returned to

Scotland, especially Glasgow for business and leisure to reminisce on the old days and memories of my teenage years and my Mother's shining moments.

Stanley

Stanley, Hong Kong

Cousin Ming, Ah Mo, Ah Ching and I were all still studying in Canada in the midst of Mother and Ah Ting's deportation. I devoted all my time to my education, in hopes of accomplishing my master's degree as soon as possible. That same year, Father had retired from the Hong Kong Royal Police and started to work as security manager at a building management company located in Central, Hong Kong. He was responsible for the whole security system of several local commercial buildings. He was assigned a team of security guards to assist him. He really enjoyed this new job.

On the way back to Hong Kong, Mother was determined to start over again from ground zero. She knew she could bounce back despite being forty-seven years old at the time. She treated her business closure as a temporary setback and stood up tall to restart her career. The first job she took was recommended by her friend. She took care of her friend's mother who was suffering from a serious heart disease and needed regular assistance with daily tasks. Ah Ting, on the other hand successfully enrolled into medical school at Hong Kong University. Ah Kong followed her back to Hong Kong to continue their romance. Their love for each other was so strong he decided to leave Scotland for her.

Mother and Father both were against their relationship and believed they should not be dating as it could affect Ah Ting's education. They also did not like Ah Kong because they believed he lacked the ambition and intelligence to be successful in the future. One thing they did not realize was Ah Ting was no longer the young girl they could boss around. She had her own independent thoughts and actions. Knowing her parents disapproval, she abandoned medical school and ran away from home. She moved in to Ah Kong's grandparents' home and started her independent life away from her dictatorial mother. Mother was furious after she found out Ah Ting had left, she dragged Father along with her to Ah Ting's new home. She banged vigorously until someone came to the door. Ah Ting opened the door calmly, she stared at her mother while Mother yelled at her, demanding Ah Ting return home with her. It quickly escalated into a tug of war, Mother grabbed Ah Ting by her arm and pulled her away from the front door. With her petite body Ah Ting resisted the best she could getting dragged away. Not long into the fight, Mother suddenly pulled out an eight-inch knife from her handbag and directed it at Ah Ting.

'Do you want to die for him? Are you willing to kill yourself for your fucking boyfriend?' she threatened.

Seeing all this happening from inside the house, Ah Kong said, 'Fuck off, crazy woman.'

He quickly pulled Ah Ting and slammed the door shut. Ah Ting, shaking from the shock, sat on the floor crying while Mother continued to bang on the door like a lunatic. Ah Kong grabbed the phone and called the police.

They were all taken to the police station. Inside the station, despite everyone watching, Mother continued to swear at Ah Kong. She claimed her daughter had been kidnapped. Knowing how serious the situation had become, Father was in the middle of discussing law regulations with the policemen. With everyone's emotions at an all-time high, there was constant hair grabbing, pulling, shoving and screaming. All the policemen available at the station were trying to calm everyone down. They tried to ask questions amid the chaos.

'Ma'am! Please calm down! Can you tell me how old your daughter is?' the police sergeant yelled into the crowd.

Mother answered while tugging at Ah Ting's hair, 'Around twenty.'

She yelled back to her daughter. The policemen let out a sigh and replied peacefully, 'Ma'am, your daughter is past the age of eighteen. She is an adult now and is protected under the basic freedom of human rights.'

He looked at Mother with strong unwavering glare as Mother started to feel her rage build stronger. She let go of Ah Ting, giving herself a moment to recollect her thoughts.

She couldn't accept the fact that she was going to lose her daughter. She stared at Ah Ting and grabbed her glasses off her face.

'Fine, you can leave, idiot, but you have to return everything

I've given you,' she continued to take her necklace and watch away.

Hoping this would release some of her anger she stormed out with her daughter's old possessions. She exited the police station not knowing that would be the last time she would see her daughter in a long time.

Despite spending twenty years together and going through different hardships, their relationship was easily destroyed. They used to share experiences and depended on each other to make a living, but after that day, they did not meet again for more than ten years. Bored and disappointed, Mother tried to shift her focus to her career. She began to think of business opportunities within her reach. Eventually she decided to transform our home in Stanley into a fast food restaurant. Surprisingly, Father supported her decision and helped her apply for fire, catering and alcohol licenses needed from the government. Since our home was on the ground floor on Stanley Main Street. It was easily renovated to become a restaurant, we relocated back to the government public apartments in Aberdeen. It was a small apartment with one living room and two bedrooms. The rooms were pretty comfortable and spacious. Father and Mother's relationship improved as they worked towards their shared dream and goals.

Out of all the preparation, the most difficult one was applying for restaurant's licenses. Father sought out his friends for help to resolve the problems with decorations and safety hazards. The whole process took them almost half a year to complete. Finally, they received their licenses and the Stanley fast food restaurant was officially opened. I happened to go back to Hong Kong for summer, so naturally I became the assistant chef alongside my Mother. We stuck to a lot of our old recipes from Mother's previous take-away shop in Drumchapel. Since it was different from Hong Kong local food, it quickly gained popularity. We then added dishes like English style curry with Pakistan flavors and slowly began to see regulars coming in each week.

Stanley, south of Hong Kong Island, was an important location for the British military as it contained their base. It attracted a lot of British relatives and tourists and became a popular Hong Kong attraction. The business for the shop was right on track, everything was going smoothly and it was located at a beneficial spot. With the restaurant gaining popularity, Mother quickly forgot the pain she went through with Ah Ting, instead she gained confidence and shone as head chef at her newly renovated restaurant.

The Fast Food Restaurant in Stanley

Seeing the success of the restaurant, I thought Father and Mother's relationship would remain on good terms. However, I was too naive and wishful, I started to see the changes in Mother's attitude as she realized she was starting to become successful. Instead of being a diligent housewife, she only cared about her restaurant and would often bicker with Father over housework. Eventually, Mother rented a small apartment near the shop and moved out of our home in Aberdeen. She wouldn't listen to anyone and she had her mind set on making as much money as she could. It had become her life goal to get rich.

I always remembered what my Father said about Mother, 'No matter how much other people helped her, she would only remember their mistakes and flaws. She believes she is always right and is better than everyone else.' In some sense, I agree with him.

At last, Mother drove Father away and they filed for a divorce. Father wanted to limit their arguments as he was too tired to fight with her. He decided to transfer the deed of our home in Stanley at a very low price to her. From then on, we accepted the fact that our family was no longer complete.

Land Lady

The most difficult process of divorce is the distribution of assets. It was through this painful process that I realized my mother had no feelings left for my father.

Eventually, I accomplished my master's degree and returned to Hong Kong. I had no choice but to leave Canada. Evidently, I wanted to escape from working all the time at my Mother's restaurant. So, I decided to pursue my career in mainland, China. Not a lot of Hongkongers were willing to work in the mainland. I was fortunate enough to be hired by a global corporation at a famous German pharmaceutical and biochemical manufacturer. I was super excited to finally start my career. Every year, I spent at least half of my time in China. To avoid any complaints from my Mother, I gave money to her on a monthly basis.

I was surprised to hear my Mother had a boyfriend while I was away. We called him Uncle Li. He would come help at the restaurant frequently as he lived in the flat just opposite to the restaurant. As time passed by, Mother used her profits to purchase several apartments in Stanley. Having gained regular profit from her success she finally agreed to repay Father a big amount for his portion of the restaurant's deed. Finally, that was the end of their long dispute between their asset division. Mother went on to live as a proud restaurant owner and hired five to six new employees, including Uncle Shing who came back from Glasgow for good. That was his last job before retirement.

Lovely Toronto

1989 was a year full of political protest and unrest in China. I was married then, and decided to immigrate to Canada. After several years in Canada, I returned to Hong Kong again with my wife and two daughters. China was where all my emotional memories and experiences were developed. I missed the non-stop challenging work environment in China and decided to continue my career in this flourishing economy. I easily found a job in trades and continued my dream. Mother and Uncle Shing were happily working together to manage her restaurant. The operation went smoothly and was blooming. It was Mother's most stable years earning a lot of money as she wished.

After seeing Mother's success, Uncle Li, her boyfriend suddenly disappeared, I am not sure why he left her but perhaps he decided it was time to immigrate to Australia. He rejoined his daughter in Sydney, Australia and permanently left Hong Kong.

Mother started to live alone and focused only on work and operated her business alongside her brother. She loved to be called the 'land lady' and would boss her employees around. She acted as the dictator and enjoyed her power over others. Eventually, all her neighbors were familiar with her successful restaurant and claimed it to be one of the best in Stanley.

As Mother started to age, she started to develop illnesses. She was no longer as strong as she used to be and her conditions started to worsen needing surgeries. She had three major surgeries in her lifetime, gallbladder removal, cardiovascular obstruction and lastly vaso-surgery. After her surgeries she quickly recovered and continued to work fearlessly at her restaurant not caring about her health.

She would always proudly say, 'Everyone is destined to die, but I know I won't die from an illness. I have a strong life!'

Since I was working in the medical industry, I was always the one to arrange her hospitalization. With the three major surgeries, I was in charge of taking care of all the logistics and planning. As for my siblings, some were living aboard and others would show up once in a while to gossip instead of taking care of their mother.

I remember the day when Mother was scheduled for her second operation. I drove to the hospital early in the morning and parked by the quiet roadside, there was no parking space available at the hospital. Her operation lasted for more than four hours as I waited in her ward until dusk. After seeing her safe in her bed, I left quietly. I picked up my car on the roadside and discovered three parking tickets. I held the tickets as they wrinkled in my fist. Angrily, I sat inside my car staring blankly at the dark sky for seconds. My heart felt heavy and tired. I gripped my steering and began to drive back home.

Immigration

Stanley's restaurant continued to gain popularity, it was the most profit Mother ever gained in her whole life. She started to invest in properties in the surrounding areas. This gave her the title of landlady among her peers, some even felt like she was starting to sound like a powerful local tyrant! Everyone in town knew her name and success.

Hong Kong summers can reach ridiculous degrees, almost up to thirty-five degrees Celsius. The heat would linger around the kitchen even with the air conditioner blasting cool air. All the employees had sweat dripping down their faces as they hustled around the room, prepping and cooking meals. The heat didn't seem to bother Mother and Uncle Shing one bit as they were used to spending most of their time in the kitchen. I was the opposite, since childhood, I have suffered from eczema and the weather caused my balls to be unbearably irritated. I would have to constantly hold myself from itching, most days I could not resist. I would often hold the wok with my right hand and itch with my left. The more I would scratch the more irritated the area would become. At night I would take a bath in an attempt to calm my skin down. My skin was covered with rashes and scratch marks, usually ointment would heal the wound within one week. However, with the constant back and forth in the kitchen, my eczema flare-ups would relapse and lasted for many years. On top of that, I started to develop athlete's foot causing my skin to crack and bleed. It was almost torture working in the kitchen during summer time. Working in the kitchen alone was tough labor, many employees were finding it unbearable. Not only did they have to withstand the heat, they had to follow Mother's strict rules and criticism. As a result, the turnover rate was extremely high, most workers wouldn't last longer than two months.

My wife and I tried very hard to balance between work and taking care of my two daughters and I decided to hire a maid. Maids are very common in Hong Kong; most middle-class families hire either a full time or part time helper. They often stay at their employer's home during their span of employment. We went through a local maid agency and hired a Philippine helper. Without any hesitation, my mother requested my maid to help out at the restaurant from time to time. It was considered illegal by the immigration law to assign your maid to any businesses related work, however it was not well enforced during the early years and the law was often neglected. A few months after, Mother hired two helpers from Thailand. In the short time span of three months, they spoke Cantonese fluently. Not long after that, the foreign helpers became key employees at the restaurant. At night, they would accompany Mother home to watch television and gossip about the show. Surprisingly they lived together without any disagreements. Acting as an empress, Mother would have her helper companions right by her side. After a few calm and profitable years, the consequences of her illegal actions came knocking at our front door. Early in the morning, a team of officers from the Hong Kong Immigration Department arrived at our restaurant. They notified us that three foreign maids had been arrested and sent to the detention center located in Central. They were currently waiting for their court sentence. The officers told us there was an anonymous tip reported to them. The officers told Mother to follow them back to their office and she was put in a temporary cell. After her past experience in Scotland she decided to deny all accusations regarding hiring illegal labor. She firmly told them all of the maids were only responsible for house chores and taking care of my kids. After her interrogation, she paid her bail in full and left the station. Right after that we consulted different lawyers. The first one recommended Mother plead guilty to her charges and was quickly dismissed with Mother's aggressive arguments. She refused to admit to any mistakes and claimed the lawyer was incompetent and she promptly left his office.

One of the maids from the Philippines was hired under my name to take care of my daughters. I was not aware of Mother's situation until I returned from Shanghai. I was instantly taken into the immigration department for questioning. Clearly knowing my rights, I kept silent and drank the coffee they offered. After a few sips I started to feel a sharp pain in my stomach. I was in so much pain, I had to seek medical attention. Did they add spoiled milk into my coffee! I caught a glimpse of a smirk on one of the officers' faces. They set me up! Eventually, the ambulance sent me to the closest government funded hospital. I overheard the officers telling the nurse I was a suspect and to be careful when treating me. My frustration built up as I tried to hold in my anger. What culprit? I never did anything wrong! This was all my mother's fault!

I was brought into an enclosed room with fully insulated foam walls. A young doctor came in to examine my symptoms. He instructed me to remove my trousers and face the wall. He then wore plastic glove using his finger to rape me.

Without warning I felt violated and yelled at him, 'Fuck you! Don't you play games, I will fight you, asshole.'

The doctor gave out an apologetic smile and said, 'Please

don't be mad, this is a routine procedure.' After receiving painkillers from the hospital, I returned to the immigration office and continued the investigation. I stayed quiet throughout the session refusing to say anything to the officers. I knew anything that I let slip would be absolutely devastating for our case. After hours of interrogation, I was put into a cell at the Wan Chai police station. The officer finished his report and accused me of hiring illegal labor.

My stay at the cell, reminded me of my childhood memories with my Father. I started to chat with the policemen and we ended up bonding over our experiences. I was offered a low bail fee of five hundred Hong Kong dollars. I stepped out of the police station, relieved and tired. My asshole was painful too. It was drizzling lightly as I walked down the streets with no destination. I passed by a noodle shop and ordered a bowl of wonton soup and a can of coke. The warm broth and noodles helped me forget this unpleasant day. I questioned if I should return home and continue to be a loyal son. I finished my noodles and headed home.

After a thorough discussion with Mother, we hired another lawyer to defend us. We had managed to twist the facts and claim the maid was helping my elder daughter do her homework at the restaurant. She was babysitting while we worked. Since there was a lack of proof against this claim, we were not charged with any crimes. The maids however were deported back to their home country. Mother was in high spirits after avoiding any criminal charges. She said, 'I've prayed every day in front of Goddess Guanyin. She kept us safe and blessed! If money can handle that problem, it is then not a problem, we've got nothing to worry about!' She happily cheered feeling nothing had happened. Perhaps it was Mother's destiny always to be badgered by immigration. Years ago, she worked as an illegal worker in Scotland and years later she ends up hiring illegal workers in Hong Kong. Even she saw the ghost, she wouldn't be afraid of darkness at all! Soon after our maids were deported, Mother's restaurant became short staffed. On top of that, she accidentally fell and fractured her wrist. Mother decided to permanently close the restaurant and transfer the business to new owner. She kept the rental as her retirement fund and began her retired life at the age of sixty.

Chicago

After the closure of her restaurant, Mother decided to visit her eldest daughter, Ah Ching in Chicago. She was longing for company and activities to do and was not used to her life in retirement. Ah Ching had applied for her Mother's green card years prior in preparation for her future visits.

Ah Ching had enjoyed her life in Chicago and had two kids, a son and a daughter. Knowing her daughter's personality, Mother tried her best to get along with her son-in-law. I believe she yearned for a loving and welcoming family. Ah Ching's husband was born in Chicago and his parents were from Taishan, southern city of China. His parents immigrated before he was born, he was fully accustomed to the American lifestyle and culture. He is a typical 'ABC'- American Born Chinese. It wasn't long before Mother began to feel she was suffocating from the boredom of being retired. She was constantly looking for things to do and new challenges. When she arrived in America, she saw an opportunity to earn extra money in her retirement. She creatively transformed Ah Ching's basement into a makeshift kitchen. She decided to only specialize in making deep fried spring rolls. Every morning, she would prep her ingredients and drive out in the afternoon to sell the spring rolls. She opened a small stand in front of her son-in-law's company.

Both Ah Ching and her husband worked at a multinational mobile phone corporation. It was a surprise to me that Ah Ching would have allowed this to happen in front of her company.

Perhaps, there was more freedom in the United States than in Hong Kong where I was sure she would've been arrested by the Food and Environmental Hygiene Department. Mother's spring rolls were undeniably delicious. She added her special flavoring and wrapped them extra-long. They were always stuffed to the max with various ingredients and made with hand pressed dough. The outside was so crispy with incredibly tender stuffing. The smell alone would make people drool from miles away. During lunchtime, Mother would drive her son-in-law's brand-new American vehicle to the company parking lot. She would sell them to hungry workers and use her favorite English phrases, 'one dollar', 'two dollars' and 'thank you'. If you heard just these three phrases you would think she was fluent in English. Mother received great compliments on her spring rolls and she started to gain profit. Most of her customers were colleagues of her son-in-law. She continued business for over half a year without paying any taxes.

One afternoon, the weather was hotter than usual. Mother drove to the parking lot to start her business as usual. Out of nowhere, her vehicle caught on fire. Confused, Mother stood helplessly as people started to gather close by to watch the fire. She waited as fire trucks and police cars surrounded the scene. She was unsure how the vehicle caught on fire. Mother didn't know how to explain her situation in English, and being unable to communicate, the police officers brought her into the police station for questioning. Ah Ching's husband rushed to the police station right after he heard what happened. He was a native speaker and had no trouble communicating with the police. Seeing his brand-new car burned to ashes, he realized what his mother-in-law was capable of. From that day on, hatred started to build up between the two. Small fights started to break out and their short peace with each other was forever gone. Being an overly proud and arrogant old lady, Mother couldn't bear to be blamed for the damage of the brand-new car. She would not stand still if her pride was on the line even if she did something wrong. She decided to leave the United States and return home. She never set foot there after she left. Ah Ching accepted her departure and they continued with their lives being countries apart. Even years later, when Mother fell ill, Ah Ching never came to visit, up to the day of Mother's funeral, Ah Ching's family never showed up and their relationship was never mended.

In reality, Mother no longer had to work as she had sufficient retirement funds through her rental properties. She returned to Hong Kong and enjoyed her peaceful wealthy retirement. She started to host big reunion parties with her long-lost relatives. To my surprise she invited her niece Little Mei, who once ratted us out in Scotland. Despite her past actions, Mother bonded with her and the two started to travel to China together. As a matter of fact, people pretend sleeping could never wake up! The truth is always covered up. It wasn't clear if Mother had forgotten or if she desperately wanted company, Little Mei followed Mother around just like her daughter. Perhaps she was still resentful about Ah Ting's runaway, that she put all the blame of her deportation onto Ah Kong. I did not want to debate with Mother which one was correct, I decided to be a bystander. Mother and Little Mei enjoyed their time together in China. They gradually fell in love with the culture, landscapes and experiences. They shuttled back and forth to the border and enjoyed their happy life.

Father's Death

As time went by, Father became more open minded and wise. He took the initiative and contacted his most precious youngest daughter, Ah Ting. They hadn't spoken since she left home with her husband Ah Kong. That same year, Father had found himself a companion, her name was Auntie Mui. She was gentle, virtuous, kind and caring, almost the total opposite of Mother. They lived together on a small island called Peng Chau, located opposite Lantau Island of Hong Kong.

I had kept in touch with my Father all these years and maintained a close relationship. I remember when I returned from Canada, my Father lent me his precious typewriter to help type my resume. I handed out many resumes typed by that typewriter. However, he was too serious about requesting me to return his typewriter after I found the job! He kept an air of police discipline even towards me as his son. After years of not having a family gathering, I decided to arrange a dinner banquet. It was our very last dinner gathering. Mother did not spare any chance and constantly criticized Father's wrong doing years ago. Perhaps her hatred towards Father was stronger than her desire for a happy harmonious family. My efforts to try and mend their relationship vanished into thin air.

One day, shocking news came from Ah Ting, Father was diagnosed with terminal liver cancer. Being a retired civil servant, he was hospitalized at the best government hospital in Hong Kong, Queen Mary Hospital. It was the same hospital where we were born. Despite the shocking unfortunate news, Mother, Ah Mo and Ah Ching all didn't think the illness was serious and tried to downplay the severity. At that time, Ah Ching came back to Hong Kong from Chicago for vacation. I thought this was because she was worried for her Father's health, but I was wrong. They didn't care about his illness, instead they criticized him for having a new girlfriend. Hearing their conversations broke my heart. Father's life was coming to an end. He was suffering a great deal, instead of comforting him, they blamed him for unresolved past conflicts. Mother was jealous of her ex-husband's newfound love and felt more resentful towards him. She wouldn't stop complaining about their relationship and his past mistakes. She was like a volcano about to erupt.

One day I was not at home, Mother could no longer control her emotions. She screamed and yelled swear words at the empty living room. Her loud criticisms echoed through the apartment complex. We lived just below her apartment, one flight of stairs away. My wife held my two daughters tightly to calm them down from all the ruckus. Suddenly Mother came rushing down the stairs and banged on our front door. My wife opened it for her and she rushed straight into the kitchen. They all stared blankly at the kitchen entrance wondering what would happen next. She came out holding a butcher knife and pointed it directly at them.

'I am going to kill everyone with the surname Ho!' she screamed as she waved her knife in the air. Silence surrounded the room as they watched this crazy lady rampaging uncontrollably.

My youngest daughter just a few years old asked in a soft confused voice, 'Mom, can I change my surname to your surname?'

She held my wife's arm firmly, my wife still shocked from

the situation patted her on the head and kept quiet. Mother slowly fell silent and dropped the knife. She cried and exited our apartment without saying a word.

After the rampage, I didn't speak to her until one day, when the weather was nice, I decided to confront her regarding her mental health. I said, 'Mother, I'm worried about your emotional health, shall we go see a psychiatrist?'

I did not try to offend her, but perhaps I was too straightforward. She rejected my suggestion and screamed at me, 'You think I am crazy? Are you going to ask the fucking doctor to drug me? How dare you, idiot!'

She said with one hand holding a cigarette and the other pointing furiously at me. Her response was predictable and knowing her reaction, I never mentioned this issue again. I just hoped, one day she would see the consequences of her actions. Perhaps, she really enjoyed her miserable life.

During all this drama, Father was still in hospital. As the eldest son in the family, the responsibility was naturally on me. With my Father's illness already at the terminal stages, the hospital was refraining from telling us all the information regarding his condition. I had to actively seek out a higher representative to inquire about his illness. After multiple attempts, I told the officials if they don't clearly explain the condition of my Father, I would start a protest in front of the hospital. This method worked, as the hospital quickly sent a representative to speak with me. They tried to ease into the conversation in attempts to calm me down.

'Mr. Ho, your Father's tumor is growing exponentially quick and is located beside his main hepatic artery. We have consulted all our professionals and unfortunately, they don't have a solution. It will not be optimal to perform surgery. Please prepare yourself and your family. The most we can do now is transfer him to a smaller hospital for comfort and undisturbed rest,' the doctor said and patted me on the shoulder.

He looked me in the eye to access my emotions. I let out a sigh, thanked him for his time and left the room.

Father was still in high spirits when I visited him in his ward. My heart was aching as I tried to keep smiling, I kept quiet and listened to his stories. I had no option but to accept his diagnosis and hope for the best. On my way back to my office, my Father's condition clouded my mind. I didn't want to give up so easily. Perhaps my colleagues and doctor friends would have different suggestions. It didn't matter if it was Western or Chinese medicine as long as it could help save his life. I called all my colleagues in Guangzhou and Beijing, some of them managed to arrange a doctor's appointment with some local professors. As long as Father was willing, we could try to see a famous doctor in China. During those depressing days, Mother, Ah Mo and Ah Ching all refused to help. I visited Father in the hopes of convincing him to attend the appointment in China.

He refused immediately and said, 'There are famous doctors in England, they could heal me. I will never rest in peace if I stay in Hong Kong. No way I will go to China too.'

Father was completely devoted to the United Kingdom. There wasn't much I could say, this could be his last request and I would not dare to argue over it. I discussed with Ah Ting and arranged his trip to UK. Father left the hospital and went home to pack for his long trip.

The night of Father's departure, we met up for supper with Father's girlfriend, Ah Ting and Ah Kong. We ate at the airport hotel close to the departure terminal. There was a strange feeling lingering in my heart, this could be the last supper I had with my father. Despite his illness, Father joked around and cheered up the room. We talked about everything and avoided the ugly memories of the past. Unable to bring myself to talk, I listened quietly to their laughs and giggles.

Before he got on the plane, I snuck five thousand pounds into his bag. Father looked at me and smiled, 'Thank you, son.' His warm smile would be the greatest memory I would have of him. I hugged him tightly and waved goodbye as he walked into the terminal.

To drown myself in sorrow, I drank wine at dinner and continued to do so when I got home. It was early in the morning and I was trying to get myself drunk. I resented my Mother, Ah Mo and Ah Ching for their lack of care towards Father's illness. After a long night of drinks, I woke up in the morning and headed to Shanghai for work. After three months, Father passed away at his friend's home in London. I didn't expect him to leave so soon. I originally planned to visit him during my summer vacation; knowing I no longer could see his smile again was the biggest regret of my life.

Chinese funerals typically last seven days and the mourning period is up to forty-nine days with prayers recited every seven days. On the seventh day of Father's death, the weather dramatically changed with heavy pouring rain. To my surprise, Mother and Ah Ching burned traditional incense and imitation money as offerings to Father in heaven, hoping his path in the afterlife would be smooth. It is a tradition of Hong Kong for people to burn 'dead people's money' and materialistic objects like paper-made car and house as an offering. They believe the dead would need money in the afterlife to pay to the gods. It is really ironic that they gave him offerings in death despite ignoring him when he was alive. Perhaps they didn't see how severe Father's illness was. Either way, I accepted their actions as a way to mend their wrongdoing. I still recall my family trip with Father a year ago. We went to visit Ah Ching in Chicago and she secretly told me Father has a six years old daughter in England. I was shocked and not sure how to handle the news. I didn't ask anything more and dismissed it as a joke. I will never know if this is true or not. Perhaps, I have both parents crazy in their life.

Since Father passed away in England, one of us had to fly there to arrange the funeral. I was working in Shanghai at the time, Ah Mo was unemployed and I decided to let him go on my behalf. I even paid for his trip and expenses to London. I planned to leave for England shortly after. Once I returned to Hong Kong, I called my brother to inquire about the funeral arrangements.

Ah Mo exclaimed, 'Don't waste your money on coming here, I will arrange the cremation and come back home with dad's ashes. You take care of the grave arrangements in Hong Kong.' I thought what he said was reasonable and agreed.

Several days later, I notified Mother and Ah Ching of the funeral arrangements in Hong Kong. Ah Ching suddenly interrupted and said, 'I am the eldest child, I've already decided where dad's ashes will go. They have been scattered in the garden of London Cemetery.'

I was stunned.

I could not believe what I just heard. My head was screaming at my sister. How could she? It could not be true! Father did not ask for this! I couldn't bring myself to make a single sound.

'The dead have to listen to the living, don't you understand?' Mother's harsh words slowly sunk in.

Tears started to drip down my cheeks, I couldn't stop crying. Father's warm smile, gentle pat on my shoulders, I remembered it so clearly. The last moment with him at the airport, I should've left with him. Crying and hopeless, I dropped my hand with Mother and sister lingering on the line. Father had left and now his ashes were scattered so far away from home. I felt hopeless and angry, I didn't know what to do next as I stood there in my own tears and regrets. I could not contemplate why they did this and I didn't want to listen to any excuse. I was done. Without any words, I cut all contact with them and disappeared from their lives. The wound in my heart will never be healed. I think about it every day; my life's biggest failure and regret was not being there for my Father. My Mother and sister's words echoed through my head, haunting me every moment with their greed and betrayal. Their desire for money and drama had caused so much pain in our family. There was no other way to coexist with them, it was either become them or to be out of their lives. I always regret leaving the responsibility to Ah Mo, I shouldn't have trusted him. I should've handled my Father's funeral personally. I could not forgive myself or my family.

The death of my Father had influenced me greatly, I quit my high paying job three years later and concentrated on my life. I changed the way I viewed the meaning of life. I became a true believer in God and believe he has plans for all of us. The sufferings I had encountered will only make me stronger for the future. Many years later, a friend of my mother told me how much she regretted her actions and what she did to Father's ashes. In the Guanyin Temple in Stanley, she made a cenotaph for Father and reserved hers right next to his. I really didn't understand her actions. She hated her ex-husband, but was willing to be buried with him in the afterlife. She is truly a mystery to me even now.

Memorial Garden of Rest in London Cemetery

Retirement

After Father's death I didn't see Mother for almost three years. Her life was thriving in China and she purchased a villa with three floors in the Country Garden of Shunde, Guangdong of China. She hired a local maid to obey all her commands. Her life was rich and quiet and she began to build a network of friends nearby. She even bought a small electric golf cart to drive around the neighborhood. She would greet her friends and drive her dog around the streets. To keep her cash flowing, her banker in Hong Kong advised her to invest in stocks, currencies and various funds. With her constant investments she easily earned more than enough for her retirement.

Country Garden was a beautiful community with five-star facilities including swimming pools, club house, parks and Chinese restaurants. All of them are offered to the residents and their families. Mother gradually made many friends from Guangdong and Hong Kong, most of them are enjoying retirement. They would gather together to talk about their past precious memories and show off their children's successful careers. On weekends, Mother loved to host parties at her villa and serve relatives and friends a big feast. She would turn on the karaoke and sing with her retired friends. She also showed off her cooking skills and offered different fast foods she was once famous for. Her special spring rolls, curry rice, fried chicken and egg fried rice were the favorite amongst her friends. I was glad to hear she was enjoying her retirement without any trouble.

Retirement in China

After a few years of not communicating, I finally met her again. I would bring my family with me to visit her at least twice a year. Perhaps it was my Mother's personality, both of my daughters were often reluctant to visit her. My wife too, would be awkward around Mother, just like Ah Kong, Mother would always find flaws and criticize my wife. She didn't think my wife was a good fit for me, but after two very well-behaved adorable grandchildren, Mother would hold back her criticism as much as she could. Every time I visited, she would lecture me and treat me like a child. I never understood why she couldn't just be happy and not criticize others. This was probably a habit she could not change. She would also expect more from others and believed she was the victim of their negligence. As I said before she had the tendency to self-pity in her miserable life!

Nothing had changed after three years of no contact, Mother

continued to blame and criticize my actions. She believed I was not filial to her, whereas I believe her definition of being filial is wrong. I should not be her personal servant and obey all her commands. I disagreed with a lot of her points of view and to her that was disrespect and disobeying her orders. I continued this relationship even with all the verbal criticism as I believe to be filial you have to take care of your elders and keep them company. I still believe I have the right to refuse if the request is unreasonable or unethical. The importance is not to blindly obey but to maintain a harmonious relationship. Parents are not always correct in everything, what my mother wanted was for her children to blindly obey. This is something I would never be able to give her. I have long abandoned that route and have a mind of my own. She should have to accept the way I handled our relationship. Living happily in China, Mother didn't lose the habit of complaining. She expected a call every day from her granddaughters and son even though I had to work late hours to make a living for my family. After Father's death, I decided to open my own business. I told Mother about my decision and she neither supported or encouraged me. All she said was, 'You have to live on your own, so pull yourself together! Don't lose all your money, I am too old to help you.' I wasn't shocked by her response, I nodded and remained silent. I never expected her support, but there were days I wished for it. I was forty-eight years old that year, with determination like my Mother, I started my business and became an entrepreneur. Despite Mother's neglect and lack of support, I am still determined to search for my own path with cigarettes and whisky to strengthen my courage.

    Of course, peace didn't last forever in this family. When the global financial crisis began to hit in 2008, Ah Ching's investments were heavily impacted. Markets started to drop and Ah Ching's property investments in Chicago dropped with it. Almost all property investors had to back away and quickly sold their property at a loss. Losing all her investments in one day, Ah Ching turned to Mother for help. From then on, Mother's peaceful retirement life came to an end. She started to view money as more important than her family. She guarded her money tightly and wouldn't help Ah Ching. They fought over and over and with the stressful environment, Ah Ching was depressed and later diagnosed with breast cancer. Both physical and mental stress tormented Ah Ching, she eventually gave up and refused to talk to her mother again. After learning her elder daughter had breast cancer, Mother started to grow worried about her illness. She tried calling her but Ah Ching refused to answer any of her calls. Eventually Mother contacted me, in the hopes I could mitigate their situation. I talked to both of them, and I persuaded Mother not to disturb Ah Ching as she needed time to rest. Mother agreed to wait till she was ready to communicate again. Sadly, they never got the chance to reconnect. Around two years later, Ah Ching passed away just three months after her mother. Their conflict was never resolved. I do hope they will meet each other in heaven and enjoy their afterlife together.

Pass Away

After the global financial crisis settled down, housing prices in China began to soar. Mother's property in China increased sharply. Looking at her new property value, she was thrilled and excited by her own achievements. Finally, it reached a price she was satisfied with and she sold her villa and properties in China. I originally thought she would return to Hong Kong but instead she purchased another property in Zhongshan, China. Nowadays, the area is known as the Great Bay Area. Mother called her action 'changing horses' as she wanted to satisfy her needs with another brand-new property. It seemed as if she was never truly content with her life.

She was seventy-seven years old when she moved into her new apartment in Zhongshan. All the moving, renovating and furniture shopping, took a toll on her body. One morning, she called early in the morning and told me there was a great amount of blood in her excrement. Trying not to panic, she said she would be returning to Hong Kong the following day for a doctor's appointment. Knowing my Mother's medical history, I knew she had had hemorrhoids for years, so I assumed it was nothing serious. Her maid accompanied her to Hong Kong. When I saw her, she looked stunned and pale. We went to Sanatorium Hospital where her doctor had routinely examined her after her heart surgery years ago. After a detailed examination, it was confirmed to be her hemorrhoid problem. We were both relieved and she stayed in the hospital for three days. During her stay I recommended she return to Hong Kong.

'Mom, it's better for you to come back to live in Hong Kong. It will be more convenient for any emergencies. Stop adventuring with real estate and just retire comfortably,' I suggested.

'This is my interest and dreams! I want to open a store in Zhongshan to sell sneakers, you should come to help me!' she replied.

I did not know she had a dream to sell shoes in China! I didn't reply and thought she was ridiculous.

After her hemorrhoids healed, she took her niece, Little Mei, to Zhongshan to decorate her new apartment. Not long after, Mother bought another apartment in Tin Shui Wai, New territory of Hong Kong for occasional visits. She had then been non-stop crossing the border between Zhongshan and Hong Kong. She was so involved with real estate she started to fulfill her potential to make a fortune with property investments alone. Despite all her growing wealth, she could not fight against aging. After a couple of years hustling back and forth across the border, she was diagnosed with phase three lung cancer. Mother started to grow tired with the lack of love, family and affection. Her whole life was concentrated on earning money. She delayed proper treatment and continued her wild life as usual.

After half a year's delay, Mother finally came to me in the hopes of treating her cancer. I believed God gave her a sign to reach out to me, to give her the will to live longer and accept any treatments for her cancer. The first thing we did was visit a lung cancer specialist. He told Mother the harsh truth, 'Madame, if you'd come to me half a year earlier, the situation would've been much better.' Upon hearing this, Mother's tears started to drop.

Ah Ting hadn't contacted us since the family gathered many years ago, but she got the courage and paid Mother a visit at the hospital.

'Why are you here? Are you fucking happy to see me like this?' Mother criticized.

The kind nurse noticed the awkward situation and tried to mitigate the tension. 'Why are you saying that? Aren't you happy to see your daughter?' the nurse said and smiled at both of them.

The room returned to dead silence. Not knowing what to do, the nurse let out an awkward laugh and exited the room. Ah Ting, inherited Mother's personality, stood firmly by her bedside and listened to her nagging and blames. She came every other day to visit her sick Mother and after persistent visits, Mother finally began to loosen her guard. She buried the hatchet and started to get along with her daughter and Ah Kong, her son-in-law.

Mother had received over half a year of chemotherapy and many inconceivable incidents happened during her treatment. She luckily employed a patient, friendly and warm private nurse called Mrs. Li. She was responsible for taking care of Mother during her regular hours. Like my wife and I, she was a devoted Christian. She would take time to read and explain chapters of the bible to my Mother, hoping through the words of prayer she would find some peace. After weeks of talking, they bonded through bible stories and conversations. Mother trusted and patiently listened to Mrs. Li, it was truly a blessing to have her by Mother's side during her most vulnerable times. It was as if God, himself, sent an angel to help her work through this tough time.

One sunny morning, sitting beside the window near her bed, they were chatting about sins mentioned in the bible.

Mother arrogantly said, 'Why does the bible that claim everyone is a sinner? I've never done anything bad, murder or set things on fire, what sins have I ever committed?'

Mrs. Li picked up the book, the *Gospel for Elderly* and showed it to Mother. She patiently explained, 'You see here? They mentioned different sins that humans commit without knowing they are committing a sin against themselves and God. These are mistakes that a lot of humans are unaware of, like pride, greed, lust, envy, gluttony, wrath and sloth. These are considered the seven deadly sins in the bible.'

She gently explained each one as Mother listened attentively as the student. Mrs. Li knew nothing about our family history and just treated Mother as an elderly patient that needed special care. Her kindness and words changed Mother completely. After that day, Mother sat in her bed looking out the window deep in her own thoughts.

Mother's appearance seemed to have changed after that day. Her wide angry eyes turned softer and smaller, she no longer glared and her facial muscles were relaxed. She looked peaceful and calm. Looking at her changed, gracious and humbled, I couldn't help but give her a small kiss on the forehead.

During her treatment, Mother didn't bear any pain or side effects like emesis or alopecia. She kept her spirits high and chatted with all the nurses and visitors. We were all hopeful for her full recovery. However, things did not happen the way we wanted them to, overnight, her illness took a sudden turn and she deteriorated rapidly within a week.

Lying in her bed, Mother asked my wife to come over to her bedside and whispered, *'My daughter-in-law, can you forgive me?'*

My wife burst into tears as she held her mother-in-law's hands. She nodded with agreement. It was the first time in my life that I heard my mother apologize. After years of tormenting my wife, Mother left behind her last few words to my wife.

Holding back my tears, I leaned forward and asked her if she had started praying. She used her last strength and answered, 'Yes.'

That was her last word as she lost her ability to speak shortly after.

Mother passed away in peace on June 23, 2014, coincidentally it was the same day my Father passed away thirteen years ago. Perhaps, this is their entangled fate or God's plan.

Her hard-working, inexhaustible, vigorous and adventurous life eventually came to an end.

My Young and Beautiful Mother

Postscript

Marriage is like gambling if both parties don't understand each other well they will eventually run out of luck and any bet placed on this marriage is destined to lose. The person entering into the marriage needs to understand the full scope of their marriage including their responsibility, compromises and limits. If this isn't clear, this marriage is bound to end in misery. Couples that lose in the gamble of being married often end up in divorce or have to put up with their spouse for the rest of their lives.

In marriage, some lose their youth, some will lose their freedom. In the end, however, the ones that suffer the most are their offspring. Those who have no choice but to witness the fights and dispute caused by such reckless gambling.

Everyone has their own timing and fate, whether it is to have children, pass away at unexpected times or even divorce and remarry. Everything has its set timing. Although my Mother has long passed away, her memory is still clear and vivid in our minds. She often visits me in my dreams. She was beautiful and elegant in demeanor, she said to me,

'Son, write whatever you like. One day, it should be published in Taiwan!'

Surprised, I questioned her, 'Why not in Hong Kong or China?' She just smiled without saying a word in my dream. I guess that she went to Taiwan before and met a fortuneteller telling her your elder son could be a famous celebrity!

After many years of thinking about this dream, I finally

finished this book and published, it is also distributed in Taiwan. I have poured my feelings and regrets into all the pages of this book. For my mother in heaven, I devote all my words and wishes to you. God bless.